Minigami

Mini origami projects for cards, gifts and decorations

Gay Merrill Gross

COLLINS & BROWN

First published in Great Britain in 2005 by
Collins & Brown
The Chrysalis Building
Bramley Road
London W10 6SP

An imprint of **Chrysalis** Books Group plc

1 3 5 7 9 8 6 4 2

British Library Cataloguing-in-Publication Data: A catalogue record for this book is available from the British Library.

ISBN 1 84340 281 5

Designer: Hardines Ltd.
Project editor: Miranda Sessions
Commissioning editor: Marie Clayton
Illustrators: Gay Merrill Gross and Nick Robinson
Copy editor: Fiona Corbridge
Photographer: Michael Wicks

Reproduction by Anorax, UK.
Printed and bound by SNP Leefung, China.

CONTENTS

Introduction

If you are new to origami, welcome to a wonderful world of clever paper creations, made from simple materials, and the most basic of tools – your own two hands! The transformation of a sheet of plain paper into fanciful form is truly magical.

Origami is probably a lot easier to do than you might have imagined. As with learning anything new, a little patience and perseverance will serve you well. Here are some additional things to keep in mind when folding; even experienced folders may find useful tips here.

Learn the basics Take a few moments to study and become familiar with the origami symbols, terms and techniques at the beginning of the book.

Start simple! Each model is rated according to its level of difficulty for a beginner:

      Simple
      Low Intermediate
      Intermediate
      Challenging

If you are a beginner, start with the simplest models and work your way towards those that are a little more difficult. If you are an experienced folder, you should have no trouble with any of the designs, even those rated as challenging.

Practice paper The first time you fold a model, think of it as practice. Usually your second and third attempts will come out much better. Use practice paper when learning a model; packaged origami paper, coloured on one side and white on the reverse, (see page 8) is excellent.

Point to point, line to line Line up all edges and corners as carefully and precisely as you can. Make a soft fold to start with, check your alignment, make a slight adjustment if necessary, then set your crease sharply. Good lighting is the key to folding neatly and precisely.

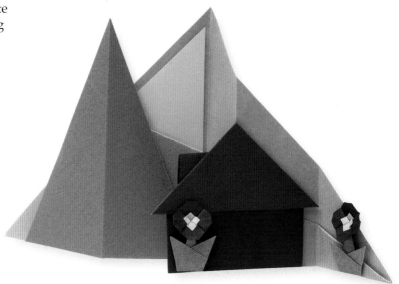

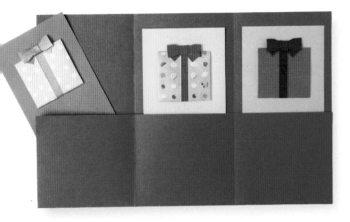

Sharp, flat folds The flat surface of your fingernail is a great folding aid, even better for making neat folds than the edge of your nail. If you prefer to use a folding tool to sharpen your folds, you can purchase a bone folder, or use a less expensive alternative such as a tongue depressor or an old credit card.

Colourful contrast It is a good idea to work on a smooth, clean, flat surface, especially when you are first learning origami. The colour of the folding surface is also important. It is easier to line up edges and corners if the colour of the folding surface contrasts with the colour of both sides of the paper.

Look ahead to get ahead When following origami diagrams, always look ahead to the next drawing; it will show you what you should be aiming for in the step you are working on.

Mountains are better guides Mountain creases are easier to see, making them better guidelines than valley creases (see page 11).

Take a break Perseverance and patience are very important when learning a new model, but if you get stuck on a step, frustration may hinder your progress. Take a break and come back to the model later. A fresh mind will often make the learning process a lot easier.

Practise! Your first attempt at a model may go slowly as you work your way through the step-by-step instructions. If you repeat the same model right away, you will notice how much easier it is, and by your third try, you may be able to fold with little or no help from the instructions, plus your finished model will probably be a lot neater!

Note to readers Important information on each model is provided on the coloured side bars and at the end of each project. The 'creator' of the origami fold has been provided unless it has a more complicated history, in which case 'various' has been given. Information on the 'origin' of each fold, whether from a traditional or more contemporary source, has been added when appropriate. Unless otherwise specified in a caption, all card designs are by the author.

Materials and techniques

Papers and symbols

When learning a model for the first time, packaged origami paper, with a solid colour on one side and white on the other side, is usually the best choice. The colour/white feature coordinates with the folding diagrams in this book, and the absence of a pattern makes it easier to see the creases that serve as guidelines for the folds. Origami paper is lightweight and takes a sharp fold without cracking or shedding flecks of colour.

Packaged origami paper is most commonly available in the following sizes: 4cm (1½in), 5cm (2in), 7.5cm (3in), 15cm (6in) and 25cm (10in). For learning a model, it is usually best to start with a 15cm (6in) square; try smaller sizes only when you are comfortable folding the model.

At that point you can also start to experiment with fancier papers in different patterns and textures. Packaged origami paper is now available in a wide assortment, including:
• Printed patterns
• Shaded patterns
• Stripes
• Duo paper – a different colour on each side
• Duo print – a solid colour on one side, a print on the other side
• Mono colour – the same colour on both sides
• Foil paper
• Holographic paper
• Pearlescent paper
Packaged origami paper can be found in craft and art shops. It is also available by mail order from many UK and US sites (see page 143).

Most packaged origami paper comes from Japan, but Korea is now manufacturing a wide variety of mini origami papers – shaded patterns in a 5cm (2in) and 7.5cm (3in) size. These are useful for making origami cards and for modular decorations (see page 86). Folding a modular decoration from identically patterned papers will create a striking kaleidoscopic effect.

SYMBOLS

Each project in this book is illustrated with step-by-step diagrams. These use various types of arrow symbol to show you what to do. The different types of crease are illustrated by different line weights. Turn to pages 10–11 to find out more.

WASHI PAPER

Washi is handmade Japanese paper which usually has a fibrous feel to it. It is either solid-coloured or patterned. *Yuzen washi*, in particular, comes in exquisitely beautiful prints, often featuring traditional Japanese motifs and gold accents. *Unryu washi* clearly shows the long fibres used to make the paper; some *unryu* papers are as thin as tissue paper. *Washi* papers are usually soft and do not hold a crease as well as other papers, making them a little tricky to fold. They are also much more expensive than machine-made papers. Use these luxurious papers after you have practised on other papers; the origami you fold from them will be very special and unique.

ILLUSTRATIONS IN THE PROJECTS

In order to make the illustrations in each project clear, the paper is described as having a 'white' side and a 'coloured' side. Of course, depending on the type of paper you choose for a project, the actual colours may be different.

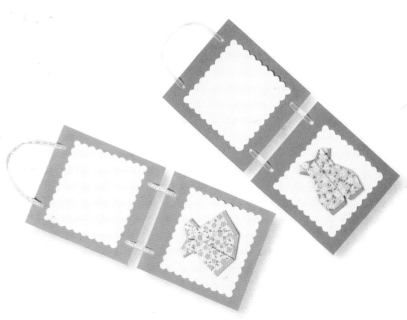

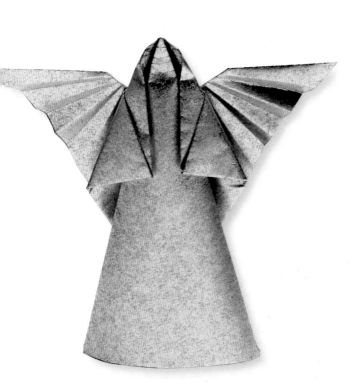

PAPER POT-POURRI

The wide variety of papers available today can be a visual and tactile delight. Keep on the lookout for unique papers to use for your origami greetings. Even those that are too soft or too stiff for folding often make good background papers. Here are some papers to try:

- Giftwrap
- Florist's paper
- Maps
- Calendars
- Vellum
- Tracing paper
- Marbled papers
- Stationery
- Coloured photocopier paper
- Memo cube paper
- Business envelopes with patterned linings
- Magazine pages
- Sweet wrappers
- Old music sheets
- Scrapbook papers
- Paper bags
- Craft wrapping paper

Arrows

Fold toward the front

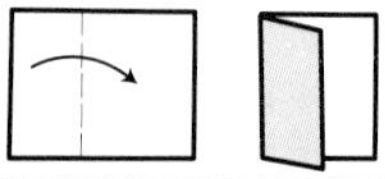

Fold toward the back

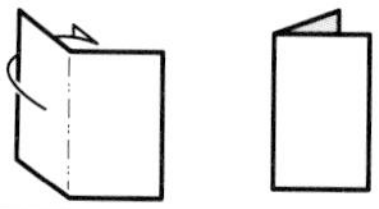

Fold, then unfold

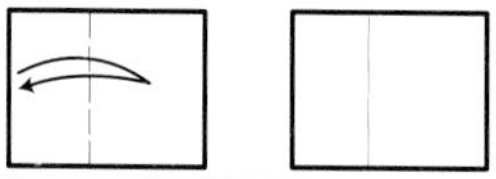

Insert

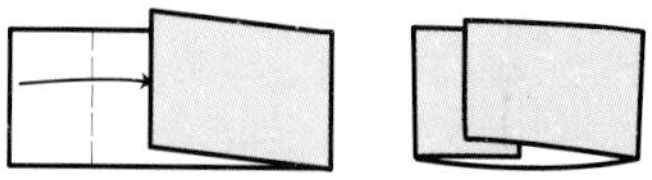

X-ray view of insert

Fold dot to dot

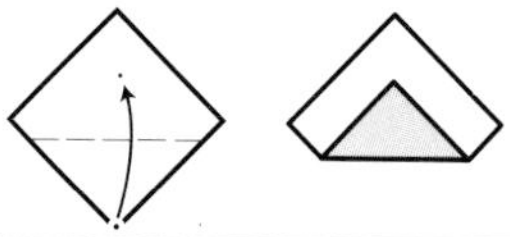

Turn over

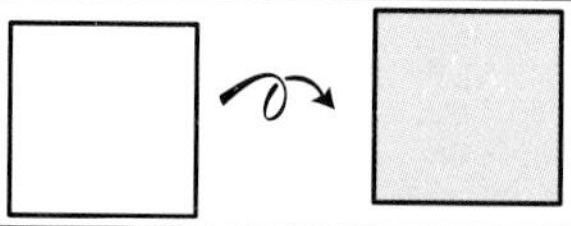

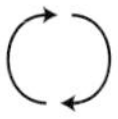

Rotate 180°

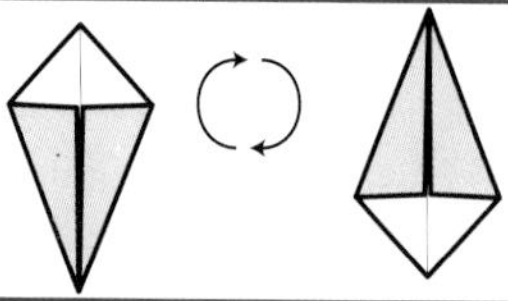

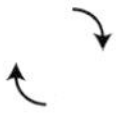

Rotate 90°

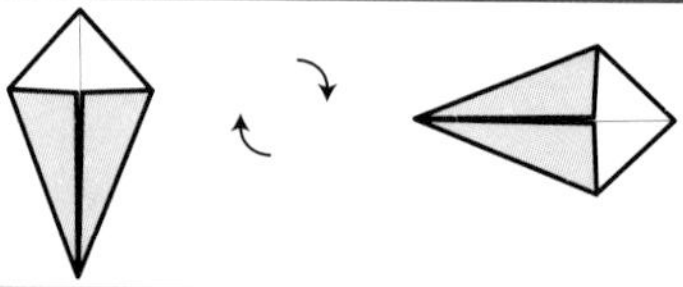

Push here

Separate the layers

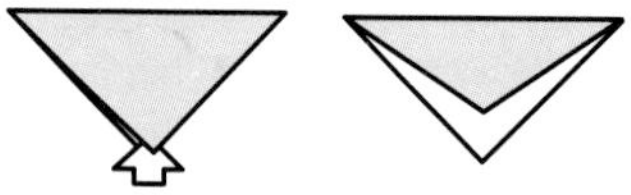

Hold here

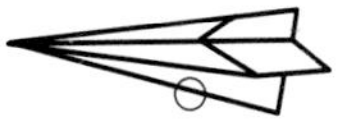

FOLDS AND CREASES

Valley Fold

— — — — —

Fold on this line to
create a concave crease.

When the paper is opened, you
will see a crease that bends inward
like a groove or valley.

Mountain fold

— ·· — ·· — ·

Fold on this line to
create a convex crease.

When the paper is opened you will
see a crease that pops outward like
a ridge or a mountain peak.

Crease

A thin line shows a
crease made when the
paper is folded and
then unfolded.

X-Ray view

· · · · · · · · · · · ·

A dotted line shows
the hidden part of
the paper.

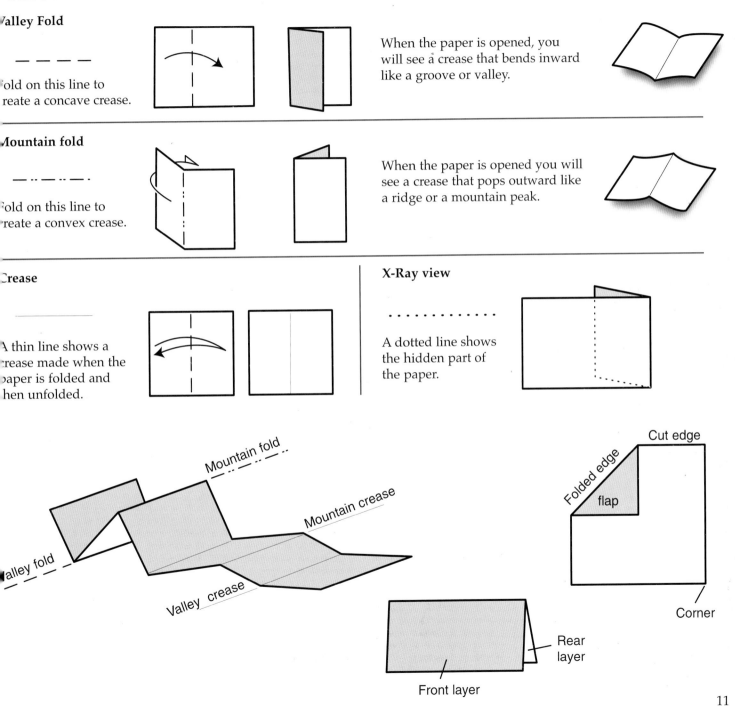

Folding techniques

Here are instructions for two basic folding techniques used in origami. Take some practice paper and learn them so you will be familiar with the terms and techniques when they come up later in the book.

Both techniques are also useful when you want to create new designs by adding folds to, or varying, existing models.

INSIDE REVERSE FOLD

An inside reverse fold can be done when two layers of paper are connected by a folded edge or spine. An end or corner of this double layer is inverted into itself. Firstly, prepare the paper so you can try out the techniques.

A Take a square and crease a diagonal, then fold two upper edges to the centre, forming a cone.

B Fold the paper in half.

C This drawing indicates that you need to make an inside reverse fold.

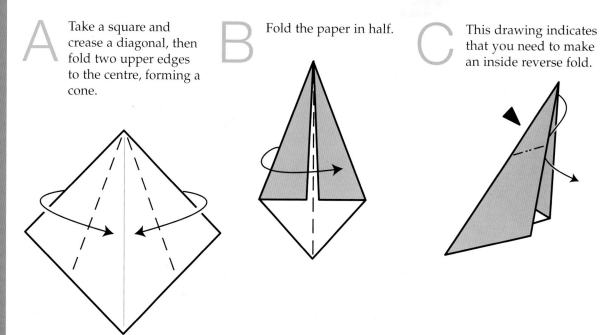

Making an inside reverse fold

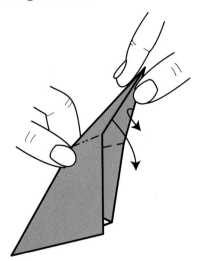

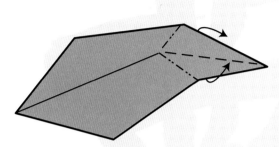

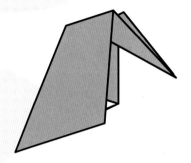

1 While holding the spine edge in one hand, insert a finger between the layers and flatten the section you wish to reverse. The central folded edge will change from a mountain fold to a flat crease.

2 (View from above.) On the section you are reversing, pinch the central crease into a valley fold as you bring the side edges together and flatten the paper.

3 The inside reverse fold is complete. Notice that part of the end that you reversed is sandwiched between the outer layers of the paper.

Here are some other examples of an inside reverse fold. In all of them, an end or corner of the paper is *reversed* so that it *lies inside* the model, between the front and back layers. In doing it, the central folded edge is reversed from a mountain fold to a valley fold. The end that is reversed may be totally hidden within the model, or part of it may protrude from the open side.

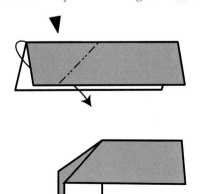

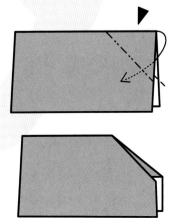

SQUASH FOLD

A squash fold requires a double-layer flap. It is done by lifting the flap, separating the layers to create a pocket, and then squashing the pocket flat, usually symmetrically. A squash fold changes one flap into two smaller flaps.

Prepare the paper for trying the technique by folding it in half, edge to edge.

This drawing indicates that you need to make a squash fold.

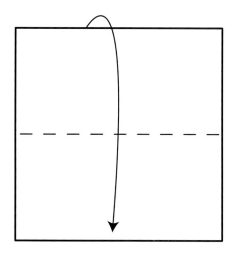

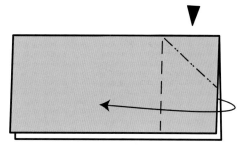

Making a squash fold

1 Fold a short-side edge towards the middle. Crease firmly and unfold to create a flap.

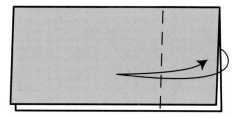

2 Lift the flap so that it stands straight up.

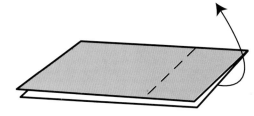

3 Separate the two layers of the flap and insert a finger deep into the pocket, opening it as widely as possible. Press down on the folded edge.

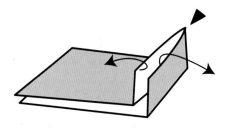

4 Flatten the pocket evenly so that the creaseline lines up with the vertical folded edge right below it. Sharpen the new folds. The squash fold is complete.

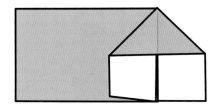

FOLDING INTO EVEN THIRDS

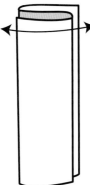 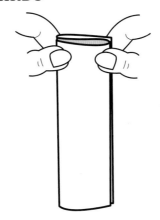 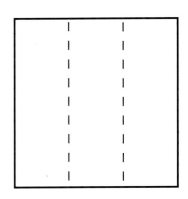

1 Roll the edge you wish to divide into an S-shaped curve. Adjust the paper along the top edge until the size of all three layers of paper is equal.

2 Flatten the curves by pinching along the top edge. Check to make sure that the thirds are even.

3 Extend the pinches into full folds across the paper.

GUIDE SHEET METHOD

Lay the paper across a lined sheet of paper (such as notebook paper). Adjust until the edge you are dividing cuts across a number of spaces that is easily divisible by three (eg. 3, 6, 9 or 12). Divide the total number of spaces by three and count off that number of spaces, marking both thirds with a small pencil mark where the line hits the edge. Use the pencil marks as your guide for the thirds folds.

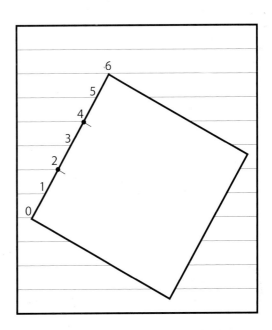

How to make an equilateral triangle

An equilateral triangle has three sides
of equal length.

EQUILATERAL TRIANGLE FROM A SQUARE

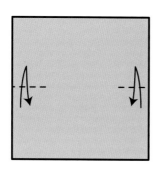 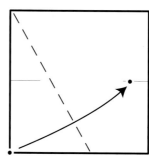 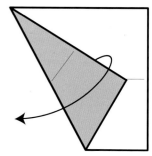

1 Make two long pinches at the mid-point of two opposite edges. Turn the paper over.

2 Bring the bottom left corner to the crease mark on the right, beginning the fold at the top left corner.

3 Crease sharply and unfold.

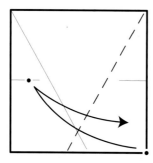 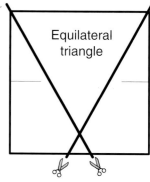

4 Bring the bottom right corner to the crease mark on the left, beginning the fold at the top right corner. Crease sharply and unfold.

5 Cut along the long creaselines to give one equilateral triangle.

EQUILATERAL TRIANGLE FROM A LONG RECTANGLE

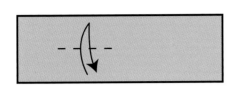

1 As you fold the strip in half, make a partial crease near the left end and unfold. Flip over top to bottom. (The crease will be easier to see on the mountain crease side.)

2 Bring the bottom left corner up to touch the centre crease, beginning the fold at the top left corner. Be very accurate and form a sharp corner at the top.

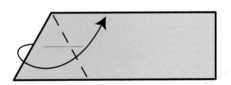

3 This is the result. Flip over, top to bottom.

4 Bring the slanted left edge up to the top (the shorter of the two long sides).

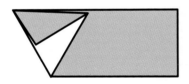

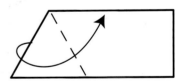

5 This is the result. Flip over again, top to bottom.

6 Bring the slanted left edge up to the top (the shorter of the two long sides).

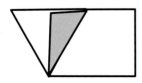

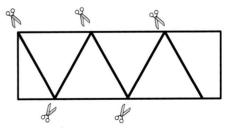

7 This is the result. Continue folding in this way until you reach the end of the strip.

8 Unfold the strip and cut on the creaselines.

greetings cards

There are many exciting ways to fold paper to create original greetings cards. This chapter will teach you a set of basic folds for cards, which you may then choose to embellish with models or other decorations. It also explains how to create more intricate forms of greetings card, such as three-dimensional cards, pop-up cards and cards with a window frame on the front.

Paper is sold in different weights: it is measured in gsm (grams per square metre) or pounds (lb). Depending on the type of card that you are making, certain weights will be more suitable – from medium-weight bond paper to heavier papers such as card stock or cover stock.

Creative folds for cards

There are various ways to fold paper to make a greetings card,
ranging from the very straightforward
to more complex methods.

FOLDING IN HALF

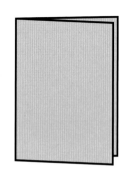 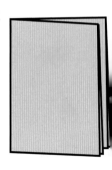

FOLDING IN QUARTERS

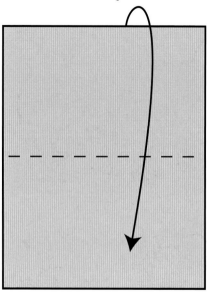 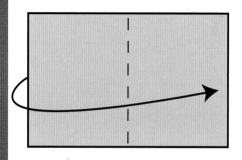 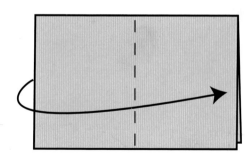

Bear in mind that if your finished card is a double layer of paper (such as the quarter-fold card), you can start with bond paper, stationery, or other medium-weight paper. If your card is a single layer of paper, try a stiffer paper such as card or cover stock. When folding card stock it is helpful to score fold lines first. Use a straight-edge and a scoring tool, such as a dry ballpoint pen or a stylus.

GATE FOLD

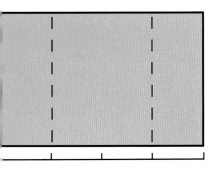
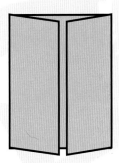

ZIGZAG FOLD

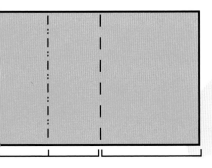
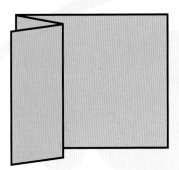

POCKET TRI-FOLD

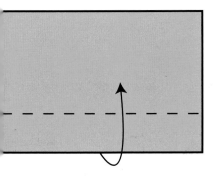
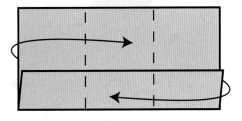

TRIANGLE FOLD

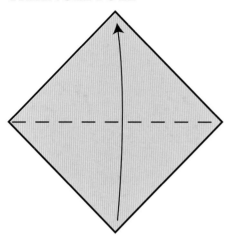 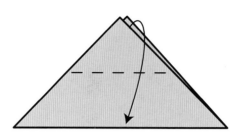 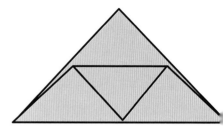

DOUBLE RECTANGLE FOLD

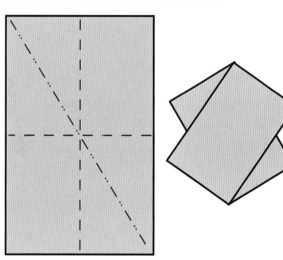

PEEK-A-BOO FOLD

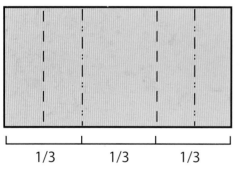 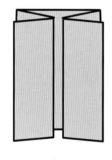

1/3   1/3   1/3

PEEK-A-BOO POCKET

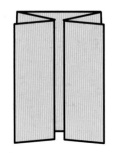  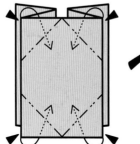 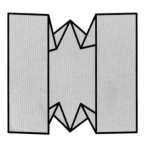

AN FOLDS (THREE VARIATIONS)

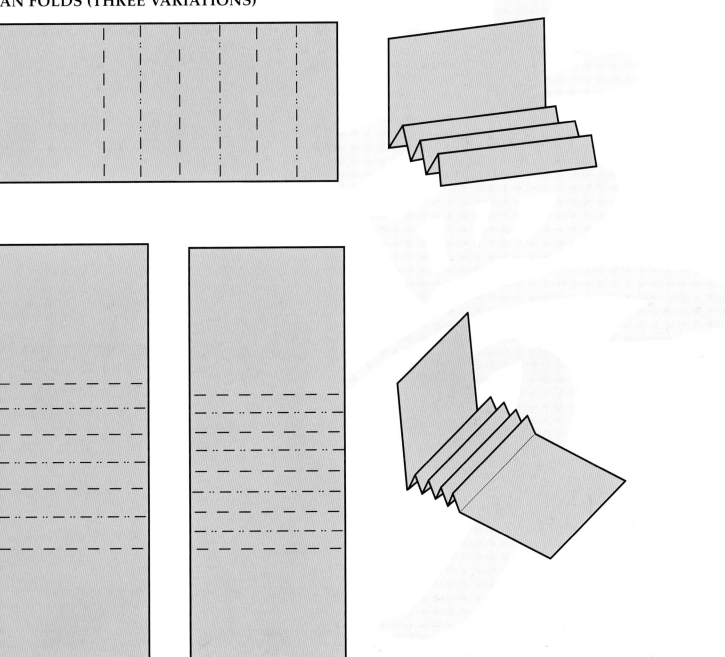

Level: Simple.

Paper: Square of sturdy paper, measuring 15–20cm (6–8in).

Creator: Luisa Canovi (Italy).

Mountain landscape card fold

This unique card will fold flat for mailing; and when opened it will stand upright. This card could be used to create a backdrop for a three-dimensional scene.

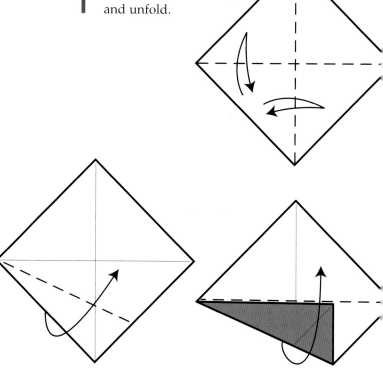

Origin: Creator Luisa Canovi is a past president of the CDO, Centro Diffusione Origami, the Italian Origami Centre. In her 1999 book, *Corso Practico di Origami*, she shows this model used as a menu holder.

1 Fold diagonally in half, in both directions, and unfold.

2 Fold the left lower edge to the diagonal creaseline.

3 Fold upwards along the existing diagonal crease.

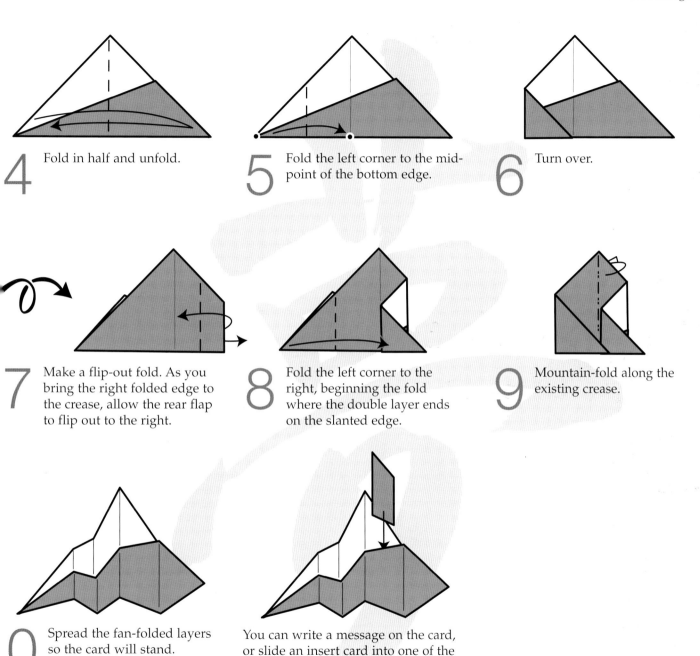

4   Fold in half and unfold.

5   Fold the left corner to the mid-point of the bottom edge.

6   Turn over.

7   Make a flip-out fold. As you bring the right folded edge to the crease, allow the rear flap to flip out to the right.

8   Fold the left corner to the right, beginning the fold where the double layer ends on the slanted edge.

9   Mountain-fold along the existing crease.

0   Spread the fan-folded layers so the card will stand. Attach models to this backdrop.

You can write a message on the card, or slide an insert card into one of the pockets.

Level: Simple.

Paper: A square or rectangle four times the size of the finished card. A4 bond paper or stationery will work well.

Reverse-fold pop-up card

One easy way of making a pop-up card is to glue an origami model (such as the Simple heart on page 46) to a reverse-fold, or hang an ornament from the section that pops forward.

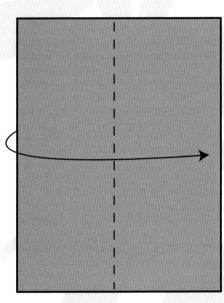

1 Fold the paper in half, long edge to long edge.

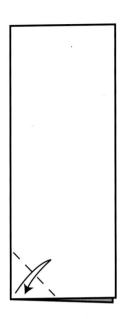

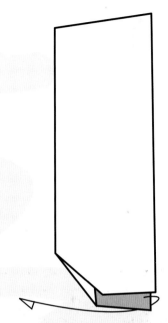

2 At the bottom spine corner, fold over a triangular flap. Crease very sharply and unfold. The size and angle of this fold can vary.

3 Inside-reverse-fold the corner, pushing it in between the front and rear layers.

4 Swing the back layer to the rear, opening the paper back to a large rectangle.

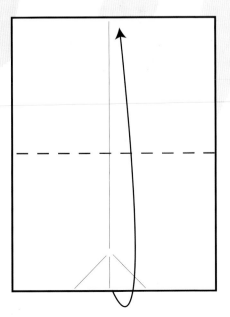

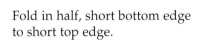

5 Fold in half, short bottom edge to short top edge.

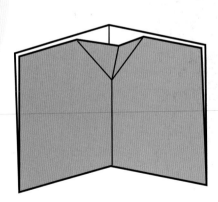

6 As you fold the card in half, re-form the inside reverse fold at the top of the card. You can hang an ornament inside your card by cutting two small slits at the top of the reverse-folded section.

27

Level:
Intermediate.

Paper: A rectangle such as A4 size.

Pleated pop-up card

Here's a clever way to create a pop-up effect without cutting!

Origin: A Dutch origami magazine. A similar model, folded from a square, has been created by Takenao Handa of Japan.

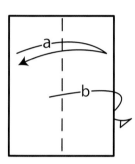

1 Fold lengthways in half. Crease sharply and unfold. Turn over and repeat, changing the crease from mountain to valley, and unfolding again.

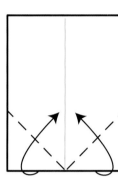

2 White side up, fold each half of the bottom edge to the centre.

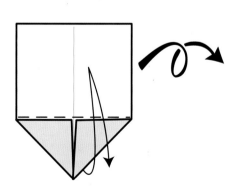

3 Fold up along the top edge of the triangles. Crease sharply and unfold. Turn over to the back.

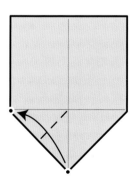

4 On the back, fold the bottom corner up to the left corner. Make a partial fold, as shown in the next drawing.

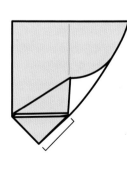

5 Crease only from the bottom edge to the centre, and unfold.

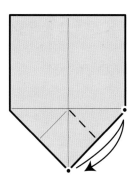

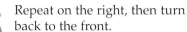

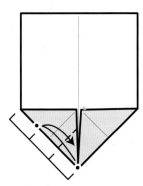

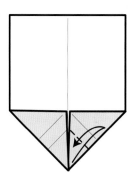

6 Repeat on the right, then turn back to the front.

7 Fold the bottom corner to approximately two-thirds of the way up on the folded edge; make a partial fold that does not extend past the vertical centre-line.

8 Repeat step 7 on the right. Make sure the creases from steps 7 and 8 meet exactly at the centre.

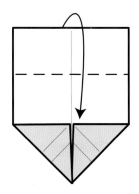

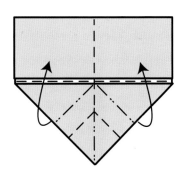

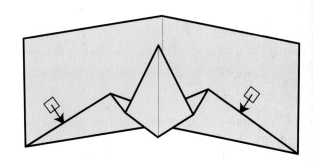

9 Fold the top edge down to the top of the triangles.

10 As you lift the lower triangular section, close the card and inside-reverse-fold along the pre-creases.

11 Glue an origami model or models to the pop-up section. Use glue or double-sided tape where indicated by the arrows to hold the layers together.

Variations: You can vary the location and number of folds made in steps 7 and 8. The corner of the large bottom triangle can be blunted to get rid of the point on the pop-up section.

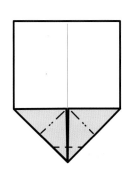

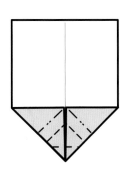

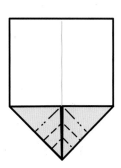

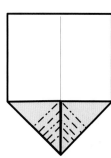

Level: Simple.

Paper: A square or rectangle four times the size of the finished card. A4 paper will work well for a card.

X-cut card with frame

Cutting a square or rectangular frame for a card can be tricky: you need to be careful that you do not cut too far and mar the inner corners of the frame. This technique avoids that problem, and also holds backing paper in place without glue or tape.

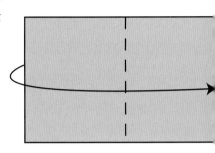

1 Fold in half, top to bottom.

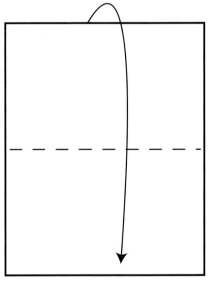

2 Fold in half, side to side.

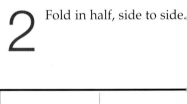

3 After the card has been quartered, unfold it completely.

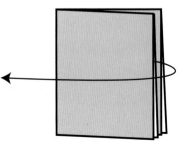

4 With a pencil, mark an 'X' the inside front cover, measuring to centre the mark. The ends of the 'X' mark the inner corners of frame. If you prefer, you need only mark the dots the ends.

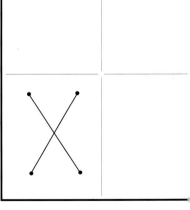

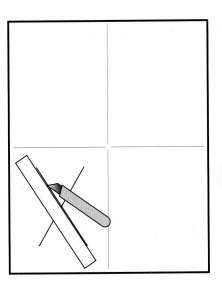

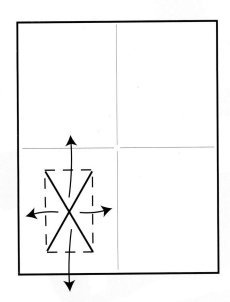

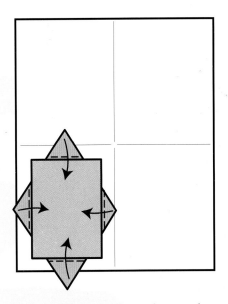

5 Use a blade and a metal straight-edge to cut two slits in the paper, along the pencil lines of the 'X'.

6 Fold the four loose triangular flaps as far outwards as they will go.

7 You will need a background paper that is a little larger than the frame opening. Centre it over the triangular flaps. Then fold the four flaps over the edges of the background paper, securing it in place.

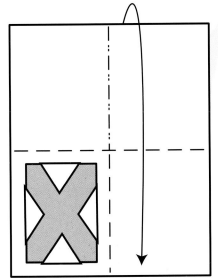

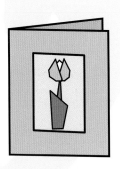

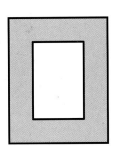

8 Re-fold the card in quarters.

9 Affix an origami model to the background paper.

10 If you are making a lot of cards, cut a cardboard template and use it to mark dots at the outer ends of the 'X'.

envelopes
and letterfolds

Origami envelopes, like their store-bought counterparts, will hold a letter or a card. The advantage of folding your own origami envelopes is that you can custom-size them as well as coordinate the paper with your card or stationery.

Letterfolds are a letter and an envelope in one. The sheet of paper on which you write your letter or note folds up into its own envelope, ready for postal or hand delivery. The recipient will have fun unfolding it to reveal your message.

You can make your envelopes and letterfolds really stand out in a pile of mail by choosing unique papers such as giftwrap, a map, magazine or calendar pages, 'fancy stationery', beautiful art papers, or your own hand-decorated papers to make them from.

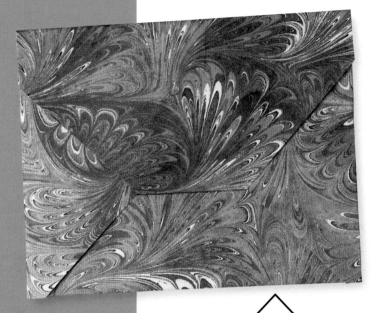

Easy envelope

This envelope is quick to make and large enough to hold a card made from A4 paper folded into quarters.

Level: Simple.

Paper: A square, any size. For a standard-size card use a 22cm (8½in) square. For a see-through envelope, fold from vellum, tracing paper or greaseproof paper.

Creator: Various.

1 Coloured side up, pinch the mid-point of each edge. Turn over to the white side.

2 Fold the side corners inwards to meet at the centre; the pinch marks show you where to begin and end the folds.

3 Fold the bottom corner up, a little past the centre. Make sure the corner is centred.

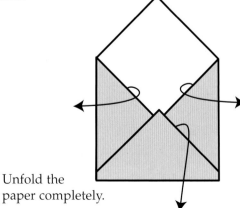

4 Unfold the paper completely.

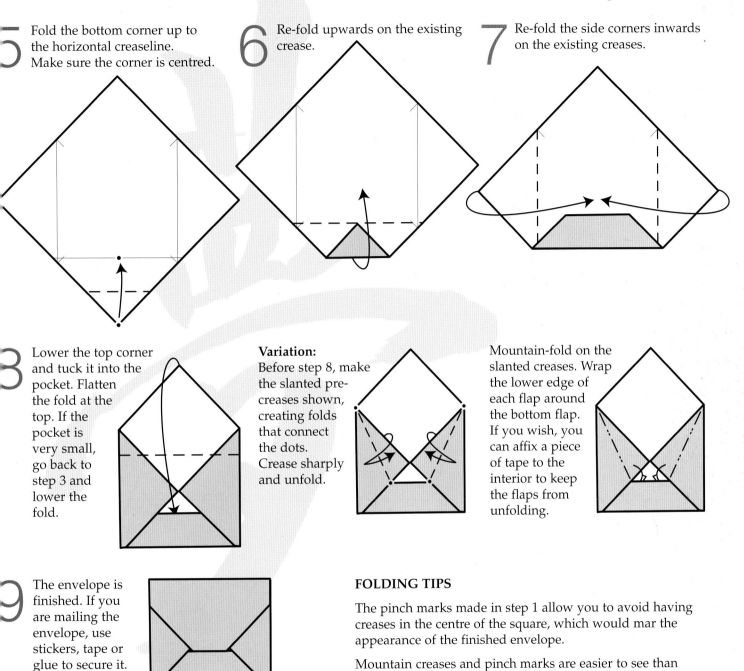

5 Fold the bottom corner up to the horizontal creaseline. Make sure the corner is centred.

6 Re-fold upwards on the existing crease.

7 Re-fold the side corners inwards on the existing creases.

8 Lower the top corner and tuck it into the pocket. Flatten the fold at the top. If the pocket is very small, go back to step 3 and lower the fold.

Variation: Before step 8, make the slanted pre-creases shown, creating folds that connect the dots. Crease sharply and unfold.

Mountain-fold on the slanted creases. Wrap the lower edge of each flap around the bottom flap. If you wish, you can affix a piece of tape to the interior to keep the flaps from unfolding.

9 The envelope is finished. If you are mailing the envelope, use stickers, tape or glue to secure it.

FOLDING TIPS

The pinch marks made in step 1 allow you to avoid having creases in the centre of the square, which would mar the appearance of the finished envelope.

Mountain creases and pinch marks are easier to see than valley creases. That is why the marks in step 1 are made on the coloured side and then the paper is turned over.

Rectangular envelope

Keiji Kitamura's envelope has a clever side lock to keep its contents secure. It looks great made in a distinctive patterned paper.

1 Coloured side up, pinch the mid-point of each edge. Turn over to the white side.

Level: Low Intermediate.

Paper: A square such as one measuring 22cm (8½in).

Creator: Keiji Kitamura (Japan).

2 Fold three corners inwards to meet at the centre; the pinch marks show you where to begin and end the folds.

3 Fold each inner corner outwards to the mid-point of a folded edge. (You may do this by eye, or open the paper and make three pinch marks to locate the mid-points on the step 2 folds.)

4 Except for the two small side triangles, completely unfold the paper.

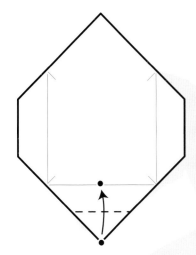

5   Re-fold on the lowest crease.

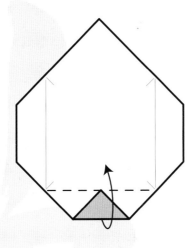

6   Refold on the next lowest crease.

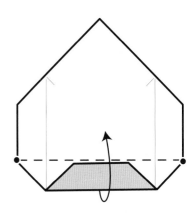

7   Fold up again, making a fold along the top folded edge. The new fold connects the two side dots. The long trapezoid-shaped flap you create will become a pocket.

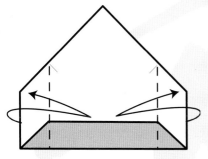

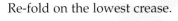

8   Refold on the existing vertical creases, and unfold.

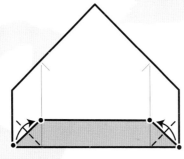

9   Fold the bottom side corners to the top corners on the pocket flap.

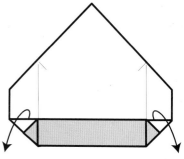

10   Crease sharply and unfold.

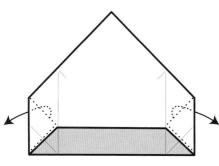

11 Unfold the triangular flaps from behind.

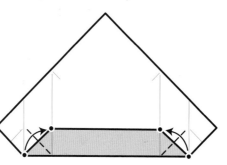

12 Folding only on the existing crease, bring the lower corner to the upper pocket corner – do not extend the fold. Repeat on the other side.

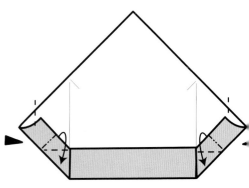

13 As you press on the far right edge, allow the paper to flatten on the existing creases. Repeat on the left side.

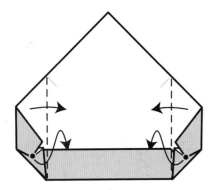

14 As you refold on the vertical side folds, tuck the tabs formed in step 13 into the large bottom pocket.

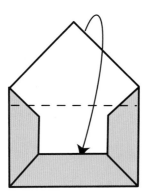

15 Insert the top corner into the pocket, as far down as it will go; flatten the fold at the top.

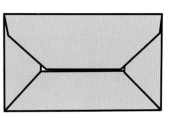

16 The finished envelope. It can hold a card measuring A5, folded into quarters.

Fish letterfold

Use this fun fold for all of
your o-fish-al correspondence!

evel: Low
ntermediate.

aper: Use A4
aper.

reator: Unknown.

rigin: This
tterfold comes
om a Japanese
ook in which the
eator was not
edited; it is
ossibly
aditional. John
unliffe, founder
f the Envelope
nd Letterfold
ssociation in the
K, has created a
ariation folded
om a square (see
age 62).

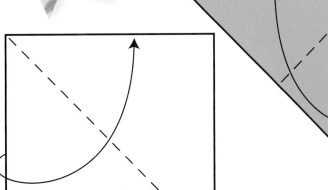

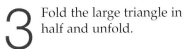

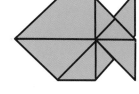

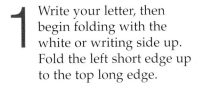

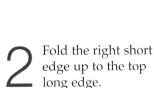

1 Write your letter, then begin folding with the white or writing side up. Fold the left short edge up to the top long edge.

2 Fold the right short edge up to the top long edge.

3 Fold the large triangle in half and unfold.

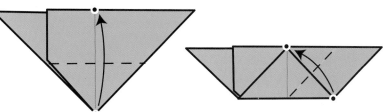

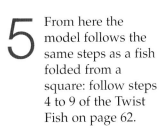

4 Fold the bottom corner up to the middle of the long edge. Use a bone folder, a tongue depressor, or an old credit card to make the folds sharp and flat.

5 From here the model follows the same steps as a fish folded from a square: follow steps 4 to 9 of the Twist Fish on page 62.

6 Enclose the final fish in an envelope or hand deliver. For the recipient, it's a fun puzzle trying to work out how to open it!

39

Corner pocket letterfold

After writing out your letter or message, fold it up into this practical letterfold. It can be decorated by attaching a model such as the Butterfly Corner Clip.

Level: Low Intermediate.

Paper: A rectangle of A4 paper.

Creator: Traditional.

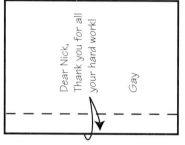

Dear Nick,
Thank you for all your hard work!

Gay

1 White or writing side up, fold up a wide hem on one long edge. Crease and unfold.

2 Lightly fold the bottom left corner to the crease. Make a sharp pinch at the bottom of the light fold. Unfold.

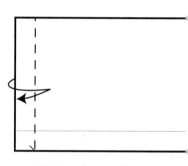

3 Using the pinch as a guide, fold a wide hem on the left edge. Crease and unfold. The guide pinch ensures that the two hems are the same width.

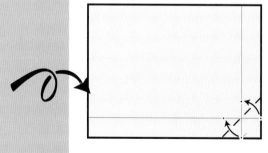

4 Turn over to the back; the creases are now mountains. Make a fold through the intersection point by aligning the creaselines.

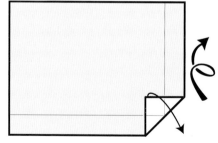

5 Unfold and flip the paper over, bottom to top.

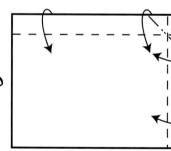

6 Collapse the paper along the existing creases, forming a square corner pocket between two hems.

7 Fold the long bottom edge up to the long top edge, tucking the bottom right corner into the pocket at the top.

8 Fold the short left edge to the right edge, again tucking the corner into the pocket.

9 Secure the finished letterfold by placing a postage stamp at an inner edge of the pocket. A sticker or piece of tape at the top and right edges is also a good idea.

10 The finished Corner Pocket Letterfold may be decorated with either the Butterfly Corner Clip (see page 51) or the Button Flower (see page 99). For the butterfly, make the hems in steps 1 and 3 around 4cm (1½in) or half the width of the starting square, and omit step 16. For the Button Flower, the hems can be the same size or up to one third smaller than the starting squares.

11 If you make the Corner Pocket Letterfold from a square, the finished model can either be a triangle or a square.

12 To make a triangular pocket instead, fold the top right corner inwards to the intersection of creases before collapsing it.

13 Challenge: Follow the crease pattern to fold this similarly constructed letterfold.

41

models
for cards

Here's a chance to really get creative with your correspondence by adding origami models to your custom-made cards. You can literally 'paint with paper', using multiple origami models to create scenes, or a single model, artfully placed. Flat origami models can also be used as a decorative accent on stationery.

Many origami models also make great 'tuck-ins' – a paper treat tucked inside a letter or envelope, as an added surprise.

Double the delight of receiving a handmade card by making a card that is also a gift. For example, jewellery findings can be attached to origami models to turn them into unique pins and earrings. The recipient will be delighted with this unusual card featuring 'wearable art'.

Level: Simple.

Paper: A square of any size, white or with a different colour on the reverse side.

Creator: Traditional.

Simple sailing boat

Origami models don't come much quicker or easier than this. It's a great model for beginners to try.

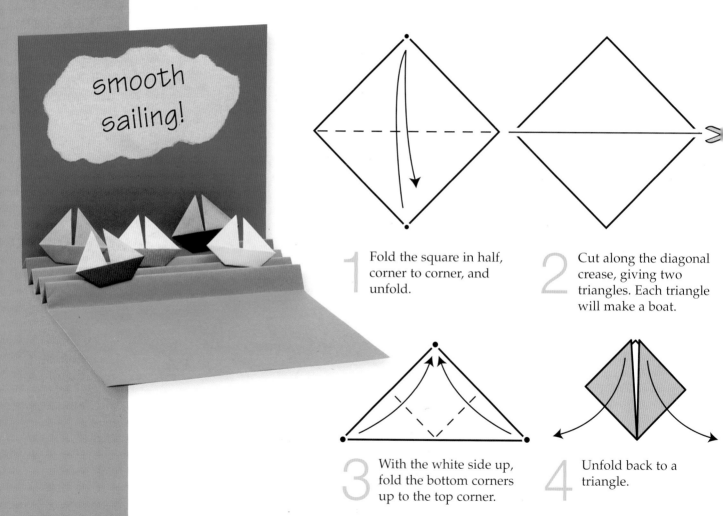

smooth sailing!

1 Fold the square in half, corner to corner, and unfold.

2 Cut along the diagonal crease, giving two triangles. Each triangle will make a boat.

3 With the white side up, fold the bottom corners up to the top corner.

4 Unfold back to a triangle.

44

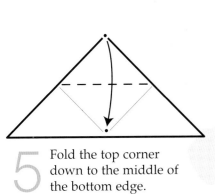

5 Fold the top corner down to the middle of the bottom edge.

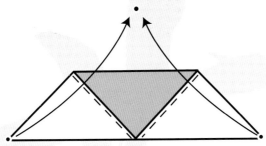

6 Fold the white triangles up, refolding on the existing creases from step 3.

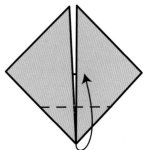

7 Fold the bottom corner to the middle where you see an edge peeking through the slit. Crease sharply.

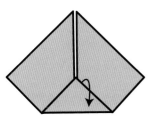

8 Slightly unfold the triangular flap . . .

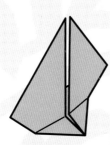

9 . . . forming a stand for the boat. Turn over to the front.

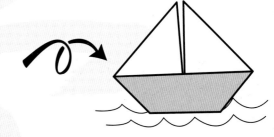

10 Your boat will stand on the triangular flap – use it as a place card, write a message on it, or affix it to a card. Fold a flotilla!

Origin: In 1958, Lillian Oppenheimer founded The Origami Center of America, one of the first origami organizations in the world. Lillian specialised in teaching beginners and this boat was one of a few models she called a 'kindergarten fold' because it was easy enough to teach to young children.

Simple heart

Use this simple model for sending heartfelt wishes.

Level: Simple.

Paper: A square of paper – the finished Heart will be around half the size of the starting square. Solid, shaded and patterned papers all make lovely Hearts.

Creator: Gay Merrill Gross (USA).

Origin: This Heart is a modification of a model by Elsje van der Ploeg from a special origami book for the blind. The book, with pages in three-dimensional relief, was written by Elsje and fellow Dutch folder, Hilly Jongsma.

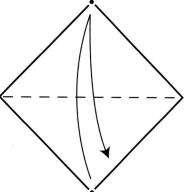

1 Fold the square in half, corner to corner, and unfold.

2 Cut along the diagonal crease, giving two right-angled triangles. Each triangle will make a Heart.

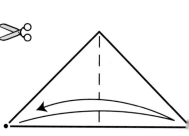

3 White side up, fold the triangle in half and unfold.

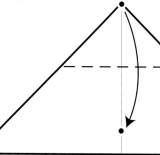

4 Fold the top corner down to touch the centre crease, a little above the bottom edge. The destination dot is approximately one-sixth the height of the triangle.)

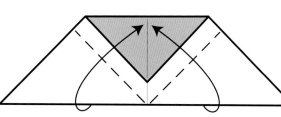

5 Fold each half of the bottom edge up to lie along the vertical centre crease.

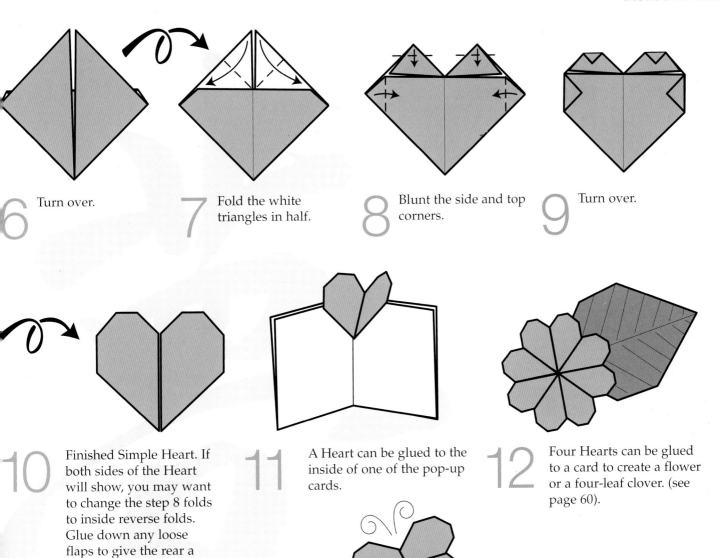

6 Turn over.

7 Fold the white triangles in half.

8 Blunt the side and top corners.

9 Turn over.

10 Finished Simple Heart. If both sides of the Heart will show, you may want to change the step 8 folds to inside reverse folds. Glue down any loose flaps to give the rear a more finished look. This model can also be folded from a square.

11 A Heart can be glued to the inside of one of the pop-up cards.

12 Four Hearts can be glued to a card to create a flower or a four-leaf clover. (see page 60).

13 Blunt the bottom tips of two Hearts and glue to a card to make a simple butterfly (see page 60).

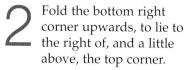

Leaf and Stem

Flower

Level: Simple.

Paper: Two squares of paper, one for the flower and one for the leaf and stem. The flower square should be a quarter of the size of the leaf and stem square – for example, 4cm (1½in) for the flower and 7.5cm (3in) for the leaf and stem.

Creator: Various.

Origin: This Tulip can be found in many books, including *Happy Origami: Tortoise Book*, by Tatsuo Miyawaki, 1964.

Tulip

Colourful and quick, these Tulips in full bloom will brighten any greeting!

FLOWER

Use the smaller square.

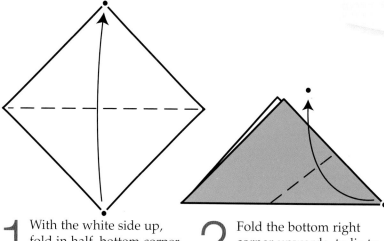

1 With the white side up, fold in half, bottom corner to top corner.

2 Fold the bottom right corner upwards, to lie to the right of, and a little above, the top corner.

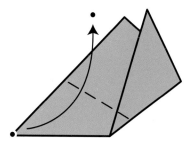

3 Fold the bottom left corner up in a similar way.

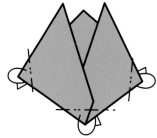

4 Blunt the side and bottom corners with mountain folds.

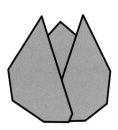 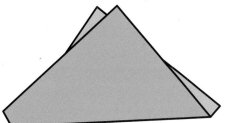 

5 The finished Tulip in bloom.

Variation: If you use tissue paper, or other paper coloured the same on both sides, try spreading the top corners slightly at step 1, giving a variation on the model.

LEAF AND STEM

Use the larger square.

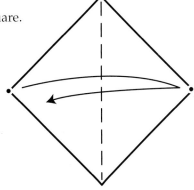

1 With the white side up, fold in half, side corner to side corner, and unfold.

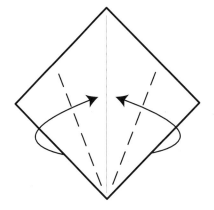

2 Fold the lower edges inwards to meet at the centre crease.

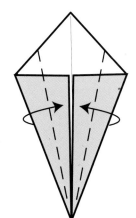

3 Narrow the cone shape, bringing the long folded edges to the centre. Crease firmly.

4 Fold the narrow bottom point up, above the top corner, to form the stem.

49

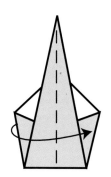

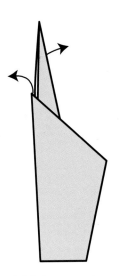

5 Fold in half, left side to right side.

6 Hold the top of the stem in one hand. Pull the leaf away from the stem and position it as shown in step 7.

7 Set the paper in this position by pressing firmly at the bottom of the leaf.

8 Glue the flower to the top of the stem.

Tulips can be affixed to a card or inserted into the slit on the Standing Pocket (page 112). For a pair of Tulips folded from 4cm (1½in) squares (leaf and stem), and 7.5cm (3in) squares (flower), make the Standing Pocket out of a rectangle measuring 10 x 13cm (4 x 5in).

Affix a tulip and two leaves onto white card to create a lovely design with room to write your own message on the front.

Butterfly corner clip

Use this decorative touch on a card or note, or as a clip for fastening two sheets of paper together. In Hawaii, butterflies are often released at celebratory occasions. This tradition is based on a legend: if you make a wish and whisper it to a butterfly, your message will be carried to the heavens and be granted.

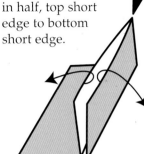

Level: Low intermediate.

Paper: A rectangle in the proportions 1:1.5, for example 5 x 7.5cm (2 x 3in). Step 1 shows how to obtain this proportion from a square. Duo paper (a different colour on each side) is suggested for this project.

Creator: Ralph Matthews (England).

1 On a square, fold up one-third or less. Unfold and cut on the one-third line. We will use the larger rectangle.

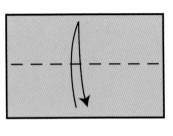

2 Coloured side up, fold in half, long edge to long edge, and unfold. Turn over and rotate the paper.

3 White side up, fold in half, top short edge to bottom short edge.

4 Refold on the existing vertical crease, lifting the right half until it is standing straight up, at a right angle to the left half.

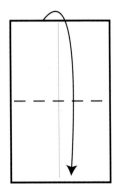

5 Spread open the layers of the standing flap and press on the folded edge to squash-fold symmetrically, resulting in . . .

51

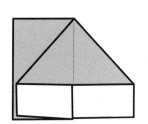

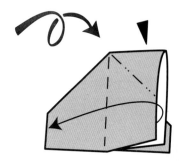

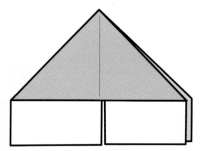

6 . . . a triangle atop short 'legs'. Turn over, side to side.

7 Lift the right flap and squash-fold again.

8 Rotate 180° so that the triangle is at the bottom.

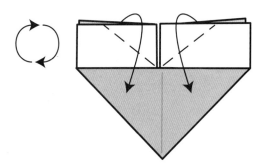

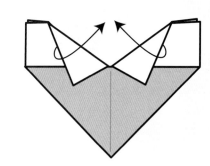

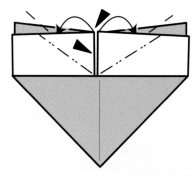

9 Fold down the top inner corners, forming a 'collar', as shown in drawing 10. You can vary this fold to change the final look of the Butterfly.

10 Crease sharply and unfold.

11 Separate the layers at the top and inside-reverse-fold on the pre-creases, pushing the inner corners to the interior.

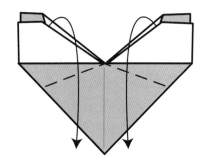

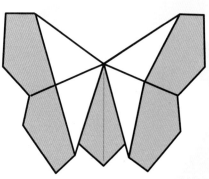

12 Fold down the front wings at an angle, as shown.

13 This is the front of the Butterfly Corner Clip. Flip over, from top to bottom.

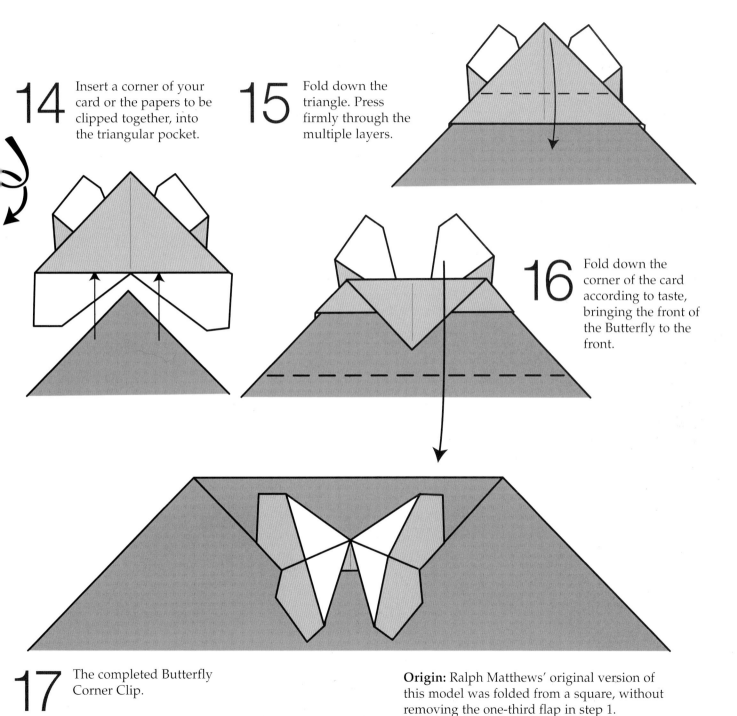

14 Insert a corner of your card or the papers to be clipped together, into the triangular pocket.

15 Fold down the triangle. Press firmly through the multiple layers.

16 Fold down the corner of the card according to taste, bringing the front of the Butterfly to the front.

17 The completed Butterfly Corner Clip.

Origin: Ralph Matthews' original version of this model was folded from a square, without removing the one-third flap in step 1.

Blossom

This traditional flower is folded from a Preliminary Base, one of the basic forms from which hundreds of origami models have been created.

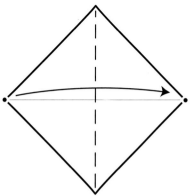

Level: Low Intermediate.

Paper: To make individual blossoms, use a small square, 4cm (1½in) to 7.5cm (3in) big. Learn the model using a larger square.

Creator: Traditional.

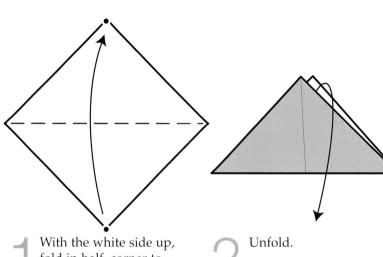

1 With the white side up, fold in half, corner to corner.

2 Unfold.

3 Fold in half, corner to corner.

4 Unfold.

5 Turn over to the coloured side.

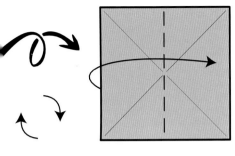

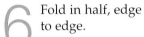

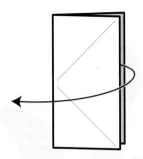

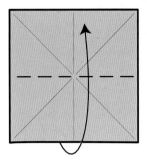

6 Fold in half, edge to edge.

7 Unfold.

8 Fold in half, bottom edge to top edge.

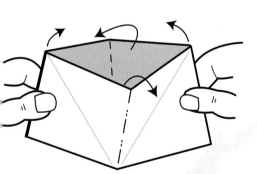

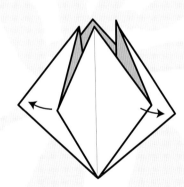

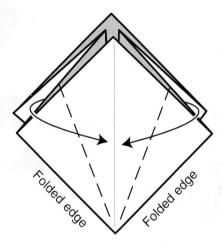

9 Hold the short-side edges. As you push your hands together, the large 'mouth' at the top will close shut.

10 Pair together two flaps on the right and two flaps on the left, as you flatten the paper into a white Preliminary Base.

11 Narrow the bottom closed end by bringing the front folded edges to the centre.

Folded edge   Folded edge

55

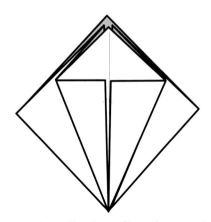

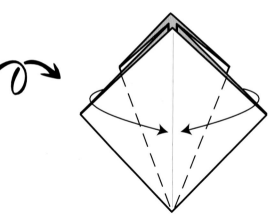

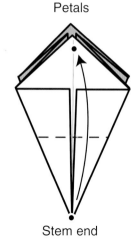

Petals

Stem end

12 The front flaps form an ice cream cone fold. Turn the model over.

13 Bring the folded edges to the centre, forming another ice cream cone fold.

14 Fold up the bottom narrow corner (stem end) to almost touch the top corners (petal end).

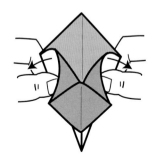

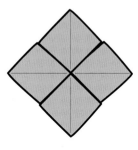

15 Grasp the stem end and front petal in one hand. Hold the back petal in your other hand and pull your hands apart, causing the petals to open.

16 Insert your fingers between the layers of the side petals and press down, causing the petals to spread open. Flatten them into four small squares.

17 The finished Blossom. Pair it either with the Leaf (see page 60) or the Stem with Leaves (see page 58).

Variation

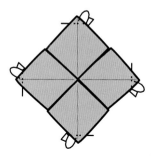

You may blunt the petals with mountain folds.

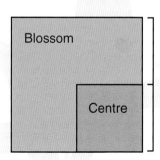

You may add a coloured centre. Fold a small Preliminary Base from paper one-quarter the size of the Blossom square.

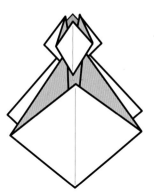

Spread both Preliminary Bases slightly open. Insert the inner points of the large base between the layers of the small base.

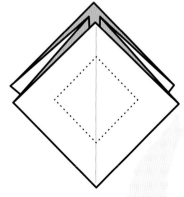

Slide the small base down until it is in the middle of the large base. Continue from step 11 of the Blossom.

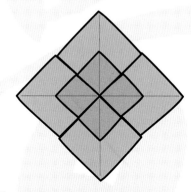

The finished Blossom with a centre.

In this example, the Star Wreath (see page 92) has been decorated with the Blossom and Butterfly models.

Level: Low Intermediate.

Paper: Use a square 1.5 times the size of the Blossom paper. For example, if you use a 5cm (2in) square for the Blossom, use a 7.5cm (3in) square for the Stem with Leaves.

Creator: Various.

Stem with Leaves

This model can be paired with the Blossom on page 54.

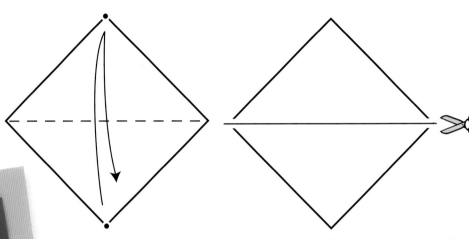

1. Fold in half, corner to corner. Crease and unfold.

2. Cut the square in half along the diagonal, giving two triangles. Each triangle will make a Stem with Leaves.

3. The white side is up. Dividing the bottom corner into thirds, fold one side edge over.

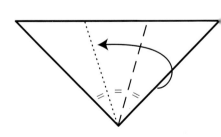

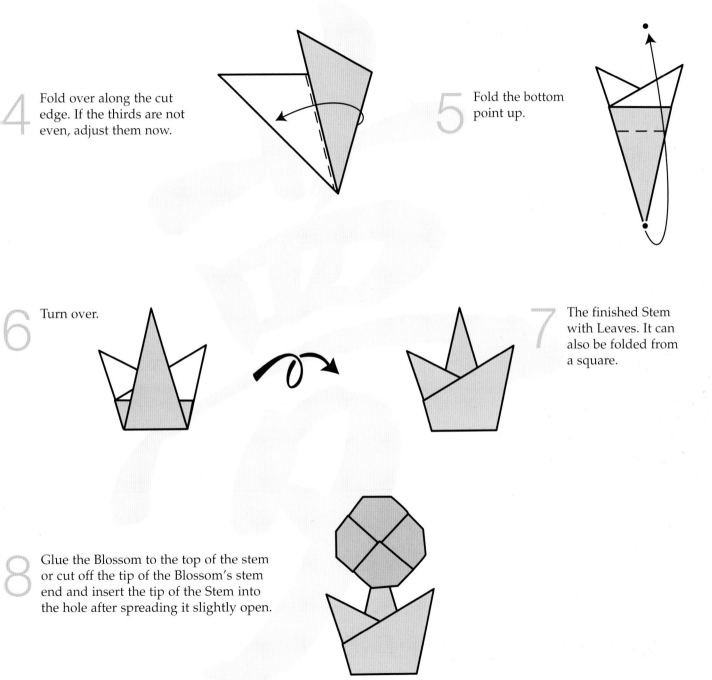

4 Fold over along the cut edge. If the thirds are not even, adjust them now.

5 Fold the bottom point up.

6 Turn over.

7 The finished Stem with Leaves. It can also be folded from a square.

8 Glue the Blossom to the top of the stem or cut off the tip of the Blossom's stem end and insert the tip of the Stem into the hole after spreading it slightly open.

Leaf

The Leaf goes well with the Blossom on page 54, or you can fold them in bright colours for an Autumn scene.

Level: Low Intermediate.

Paper: For a group of Blossoms with a Leaf, use a square the same size as the Blossom square. If you are pairing one Blossom with one Leaf, use a square one-third smaller. For example, a 5cm (2in) Leaf square, with a 7.5cm (3in) Blossom square.

Creator: Various.

60

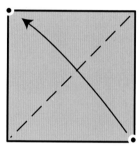

1 Colored side up, fold in half, corner to corner.

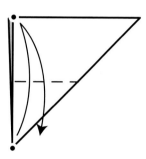

2 Fold the bottom corner to the top corner, dividing the left edge in half. Crease sharply and unfold.

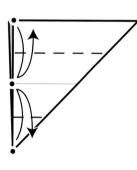

3 Fold the top and bottom corners to the one-half crease, dividing the left edge in quarters. Crease sharply and unfold.

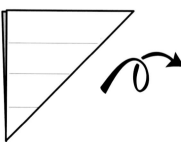

4 Turn over, left to right. The quarter-folds will be mountain creases on this side.

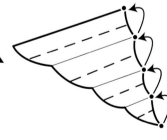

5 One at a time, pinch each mountain crease into a peak, and fold it upwards to lie on the neighbouring crease or edge. This will put a valley fold midway between each quarter section, dividing the right edge into eighths.

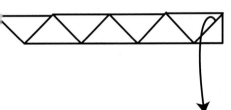

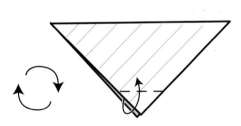

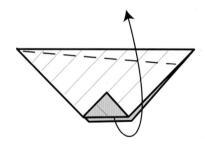

6 Sharpen the folds, then unfold the pleats, returning to a triangle. Reposition the paper so the folded edge is at the top, and the shortest eighth crease is at the left.

7 Fold the front bottom corner up a little to blunt the corner. Repeat behind to match.

8 The shortest eighth is still at the left. Fold the front layer up, on a slant, beginning the fold at the left corner and tapering it to be wider at the right.

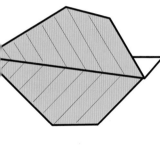

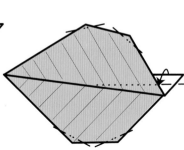

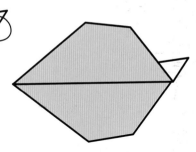

9 The completed Leaf.

If you wish, you can blunt the top and bottom corners with mountain folds to give the Leaf a rounder shape. For a narrower stem, bring the folded edge to the inner crease. This makes a nice bookmark.

You may also choose to hide the triangle at the stem end by folding it to the rear.

For a quick Leaf, eliminate the vein creases (steps 2 to 6).

Twist Fish

This model has a fun folding sequence that is also a great maths lesson!

Level: Low Intermediate.

Paper: A square, any size. Experiment with shaded and patterned papers.

Creator: John Cunliffe (England).

Card design by Linda Bogan.

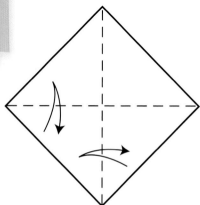

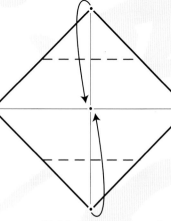

1 White side up, fold in half along both diagonals and unfold.

2 Fold the bottom and top corners to the centre of the square.

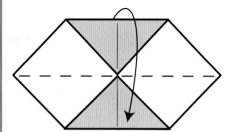

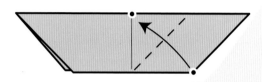

3 Fold in half, top to bottom, along the existing crease, to give a trapezoid shape.

4 The mid-point of the long, top edge is the guide mark or 'destination dot' for the next three folds. First fold the bottom right corner to the guide mark. The right half of the bottom edge will align with the vertical centre crease.

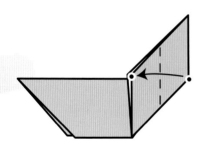

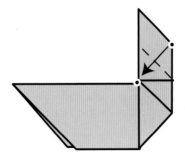

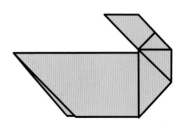

5 The resulting flap is a parallelogram. Fold the outside obtuse (wide, blunt) corner to the destination dot.

6 Fold the new obtuse corner to the destination dot.

7 This is one half of the Twist Fish. Turn over to the back.

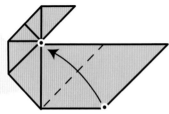

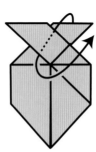

8 Repeat steps 4 to 6 on this side.

9 To lock, the two tail flaps switch places. Flex the rear tail flap to slide it to the front. As you do so, the front flap will flip to the rear.

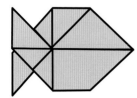

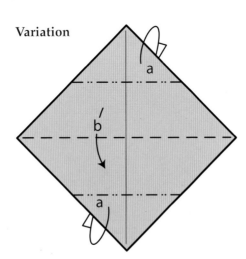

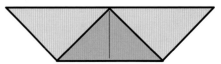

The result is a two-color trapezoid; proceed with step 4.

10 Rotate the model and the Twist Fish is ready for an aquatic setting.

Variation

If you are using duo paper, change step 2 folds to mountain folds, then fold in half as before.

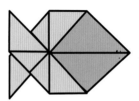

The Twist Fish will show both sides of the paper.

Penguin

These lovable creatures will make a great decoration for any card.

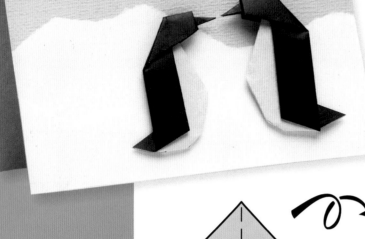

Level: Low Intermediate.

Paper: A square, black on one side and white on the reverse.

Creator: Various.

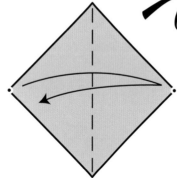

1 With the black side up, fold in half, corner to corner, and unfold.

2 Turn over to the white side. Fold the upper side edges to the centre crease, forming an . . .

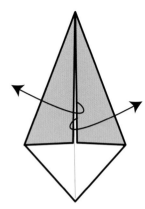

3 . . . upside-down ice cream cone. Crease and unfold.

4 Fold each side corner to the nearest cone crease, making the new fold parallel to the cone crease.

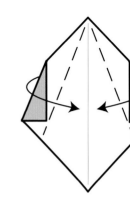

5 Refold on the cone creases.

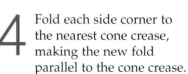

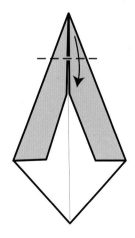

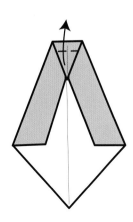

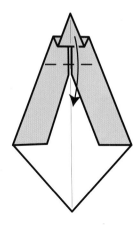

6 Lower the beak.

7 Fold the beak back up, forming a pleat in the paper.

8 Lower the head with a soft fold.

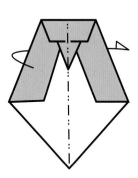

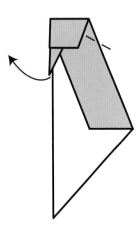

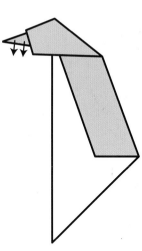

9 Mountain-fold the paper in half, bringing the left half behind the right half.

10 Raise the head, then pinch the back of the head to set the head in this new position.

11 While holding the head, firmly grasp the beak and lower it slightly. Pinch the head to set the beak in this new position.

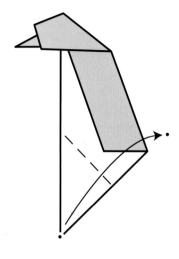

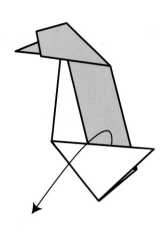

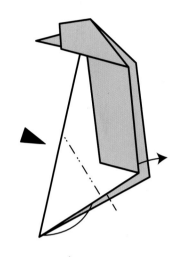

12 Fold the bottom white corner a little past the black edge.

13 Crease very sharply and unfold.

14 Inside-reverse-fold along the crease just made, forming the penguin's belly and the tail sticking out on the right.

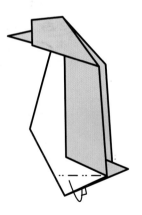

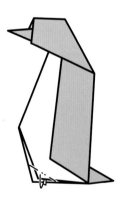

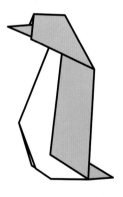

15 Mountain-fold the front layers of the bottom edge to the interior on a slant. Repeat behind to match.

16 Blunt the bottom corners with mountain folds, front and back.

17 The finished Penguin. You may vary the angle of the head to make a Penguin looking up, down, or straight ahead. If you would like to change the size of the head and beak go back to steps 6, 7 and 8 and adjust the folds as required.

Duck

Water birds such as swans, cranes and ducks mate for life,
and are therefore considered to be symbols of romantic love. Mandarin
ducks, in particular, are known for their devotion to their partner,
and were often seen at traditional Chinese wedding ceremonies.

evel: Low
termediate.

per: If the duck is
be fixed on a
rd, use a square
easuring 4–7.5cm
–3in) for the
uck. For learning
e model, use a
quare measuring
–15cm (4–6in).

reator: Kunihiko
asahara (Japan).

rigin: Many of
unihiko
asahara's books
origami have
en translated into
nglish. This Duck
mes from his 1967
ok, *Creative*
rigami.

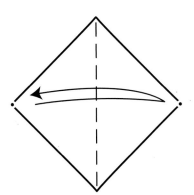

1 White side up, fold in half, corner to corner. Crease and unfold.

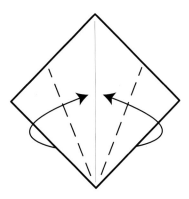

2 Fold the lower edges to the centre, forming an ice cream cone shape.

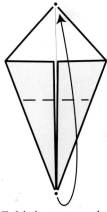

3 Fold the narrow bottom corner up to the top corner.

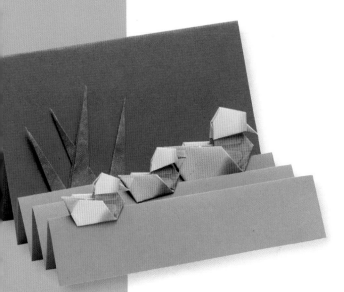

4 Fold the narrow corner down, in line with the cut edges at the top of the cone. This is the head fold and will become the back of the Duck's head.

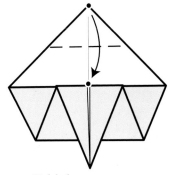

5 Fold the top corner down to the head fold.

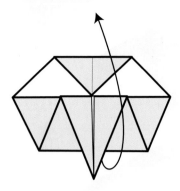

6 Unfold the head fold.

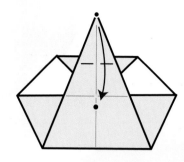

7 Fold the narrow corner down to a little past the head fold, or approximately one-third the height of the triangle.

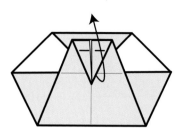

8 Fold the narrow corner back up so that it extends past the last fold, forming a small pleat. The part that protrudes will be the Duck's beak.

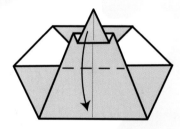

9 Refold down on the existing head fold.

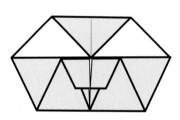

10 Rotate the paper so that the head points left.

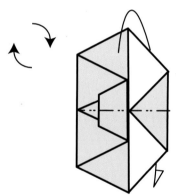

11 Mountain-fold in half, folding the top half behind the bottom half.

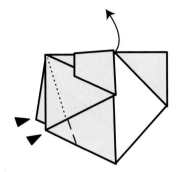

12 Push on the front edges to raise the neck upwards to the position shown in drawing 13. Pinch the base of the neck to set it in the new position.

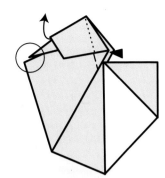

13 Hold the beak firmly to prevent it from moving. With your other hand, push on the back edges of the head, causing the forehead to rise higher than the beak.

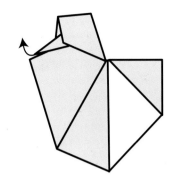

14 Lift the beak slightly and pinch the front of the head to set the beak in the new position.

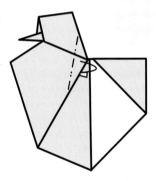

15 Mountain-fold the back of the neck. Repeat behind.

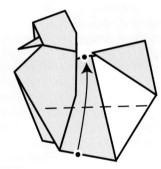

16 Fold the short bottom edge up to lie along the top edge of the body. Repeat behind.

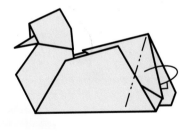

17 Mountain-fold the right edge to the interior, at a suitable angle. Repeat behind.

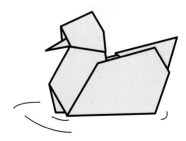

18 The finished Duck. Fold a mate or some ducklings to swim with it.

Level: Simple.

Paper: A small square of duo paper, approximately 5cm (2in) to 7.5cm (3in) big.

Creator: Traditional.

Handbag

This Handbag holds a mini handkerchief containing a message. You can team up the Handbag with the Hat (page 76), Party Dress (page 78) or Two-tone Dress (page 82), making them in matching colours.

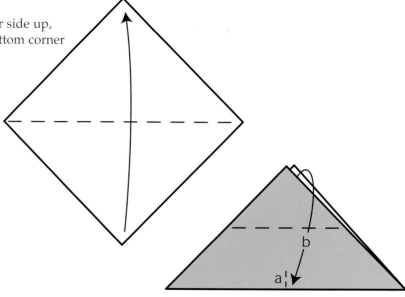

1 With the colour side up, fold in half, bottom corner to top corner.

2 a) Pinch the mid-point of the bottom edge.
b) Fold the top corner, front layer only, down to the mid-point of the bottom edge.

Card design by Sok Song.

3 Unfold the triangular flap.

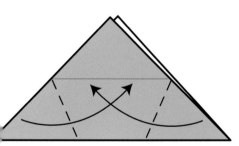

4 Fold the lower section of each slanted side edge upwards to lie along the horizontal crease. The flaps will overlap.

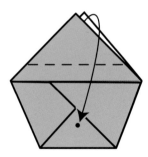

5 Fold down the top corner, front layer only, to a little below the spot where the flaps cross each other.

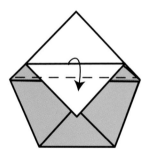

6 Fold down a narrow band along the existing crease.

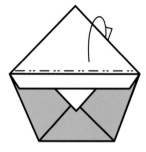

7 Mountain-fold the top triangle to the rear.

8 Blunt the top corners with mountain folds. Crease very sharply and unfold. Reverse-fold the top corners to the interior.

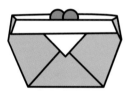

9 If you wish to add a clasp, use a hole punch to make two small circles. Glue them together, then glue them to the top edge of the bag.

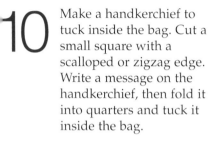

10 Make a handkerchief to tuck inside the bag. Cut a small square with a scalloped or zigzag edge. Write a message on the handkerchief, then fold it into quarters and tuck it inside the bag.

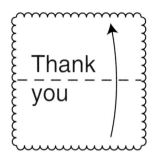

Thank you

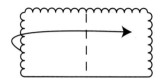

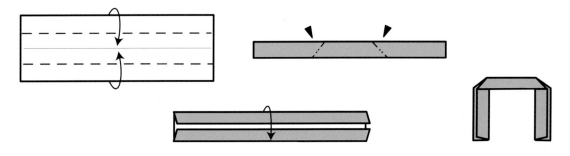

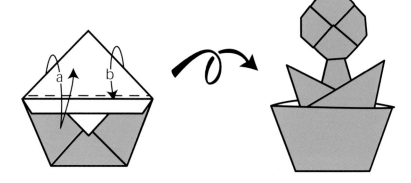

11 If you wish, make a handle. Narrow a thin strip.
Reverse-fold it into a handle shape and attach it
inside the bag.

Variations

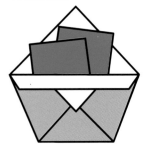

If you omit steps 7 and 8, you can use
the model as a Paper Pocket.

To make a flowerpot, fold the
triangular flap down and back up.
Then tuck the flap into the pocket.

Turn the model over and you have a
flowerpot. If you mountain-fold the
bottom edge of the flowerpot up to
the rear of the top edge, you can use
the resulting shallow 'dish' on a card,
as a candle holder.

Origin: This is a variation on the
traditional paper cup. It appears in
Happy Origami – Tortoise Book, from
1964.

Get Well
Soon!

*This delightful flowerpot can
be decorated with a message
and sent to a friend to cheer
them up!*

Santa

This distinctive Santa will stand out from the crowd of mass-produced Christmas cards on the mantlepiece. The head can be used on its own – a card with multiple Satnta heads would be very effective.

evel: Low
ntermediate.

aper: Two squares
f equal size, red on
ne side, white on
ie reverse.

reator: Yasuhiro
ano and Masao
lizuno (Japan).

HEAD

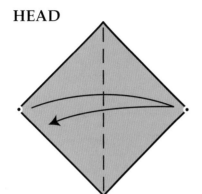

1 Red side up, fold in half, corner to corner, and unfold.

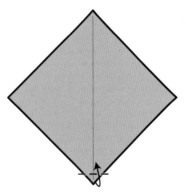

2 Fold the bottom corner up to form a very tiny white triangle. This will be the pom-pom on Santa's hat.

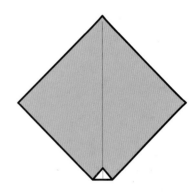

3 Turn over to the white side.

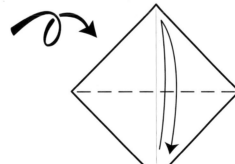

4 Fold in half along the diagonal, crease sharply in the mid-section and unfold.

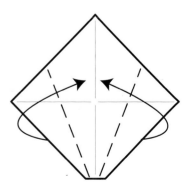

5 Fold the lower edges to the centre crease.

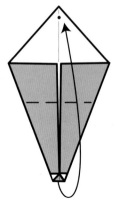

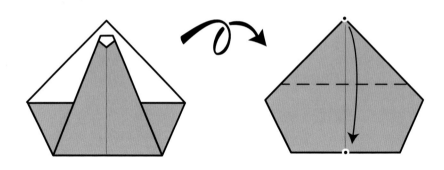

6 Fold the bottom up to a little below the top corner, refolding on the crease made in step 4.

7 Turn over, side to side.

8 Fold the top corner down to the mid-point of the bottom edge.

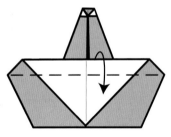

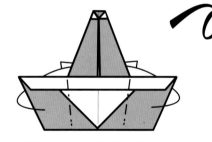

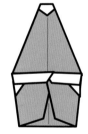

9 Fold the white edge down to create the band on Santa's hat.

10 Mountain-fold the sides to the rear, and turn over.

11 If the flaps overlap a little, you can tuck one corner of the band into the other as shown. Turn back to the front.

12 Fold Santa's hat down at an angle.

13 Santa's head is ready to be joined to the body. The top edge of the body will slide behind Santa's beard.

You can attach a mini santa to coloured paper to make a lovely tree decoration or gift tag, complete with silk ribbon.

BODY

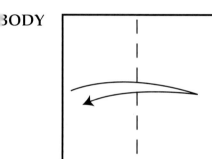

1 White side up, fold in half, side edge to side edge, and unfold.

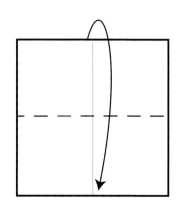

2 Fold in half, top edge to bottom edge.

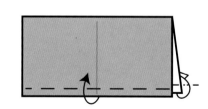

3 Fold up a narrow white hem along the front bottom edge. Repeat behind to match.

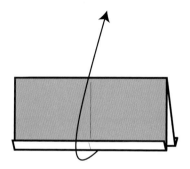

4 Lift the front layer.

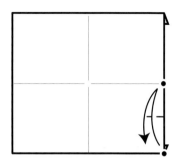

5 Bring the bottom corner up to the middle crease, pinch and unfold.

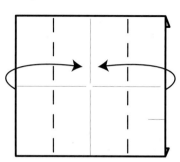

6 Fold the side, cut edges to the centre crease.

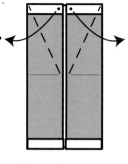

7 Place a finger under the middle creaselines. Lift the loose inner corners at the top edge and fold them outwards, creating a white collar.

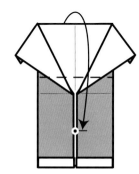

8 Fold the top edge down to the pinch mark made in step 5. Crease sharply.

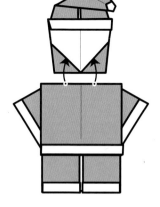

9 Santa's suit is complete. Slide the top edge under Santa's beard.

10 Santa is ready to spread Christmas cheer!

Hat

Coordinate the Hat with one of the dresses,
or use it on its own to congratulate
someone with a 'Hats Off!' message.

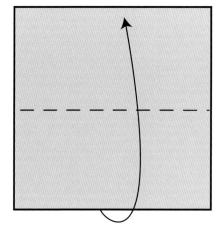

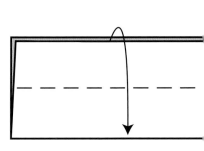

*Card design by Sok Song
and Gay Merrill Gross.*

Level: Simple.

Paper: One square,
any size. The
finished Hat will be
as wide as
the starting square.

Creator: Gay
Merrill Gross
(USA).

1 Coloured side up, fold in
half, bottom edge to top
edge.

2 Fold the top edge, front
layer only, down to the
bottom.

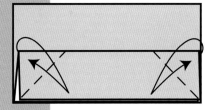

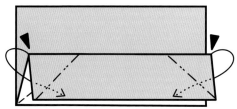

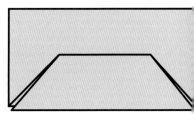

3 Fold the mid-line
corners down to bottom
edge. Crease extra
sharply and unfold.

4 Inside-reverse-fold on
the creases just made,
inverting the corners
between the layers.

5 Turn over to the back.

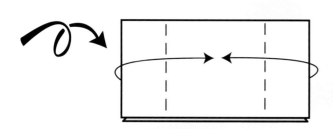

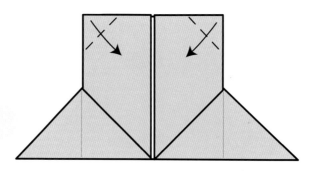

6 Fold the side edges to the middle, leaving behind the bottom points from the rear layer.

7 Blunt the top corners.

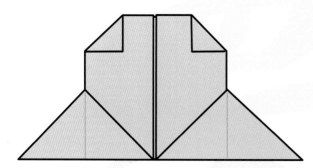

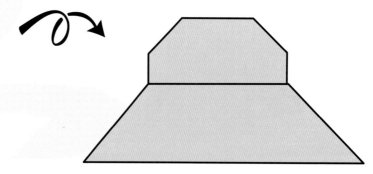

8 Turn over.

9 The finished Hat. Dress it up with a band, a bow (see page 84), or a Florette (see page 91).

Variation

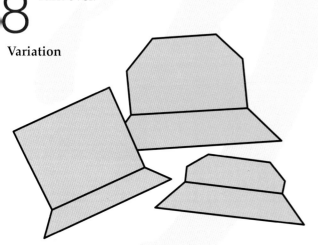

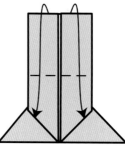

Using a square or a rectangle, you can change the size of the flap folded up at step 1. This will allow you to create Hats of different proportions.

If you make the Hat from a 2:3 rectangle, and make step 1 a one-third fold instead of one-half, it produces a very tall top section after step 7. Tuck the top corners into the bottom pockets. This method gives a Hat with a more finished edge at the top. Blunt the top corners, as before.

Party dress

Here's a lovely way to truly 'dress up' a card!

Card design by MaryAnn Scheblein-Dawson.

Level: Intermediate.

Paper: A square measuring approximately 13cm (5in).

Creator: Alison Reisel (USA).

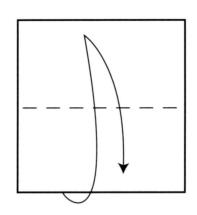

1 White side up, fold in half, bottom edge to top edge, crease and unfold.

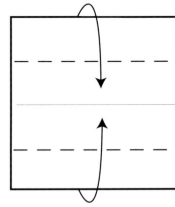

2 Fold the top and bottom edges to the centre crease.

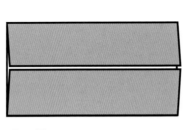

3 Turn over.

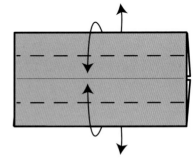

4 Make a flip-out fold. As you bring the long folded edges to the centre, allow the flaps from the rear to escape and flip outwards.

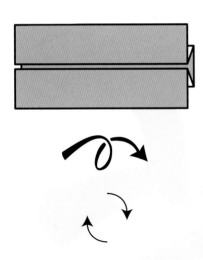

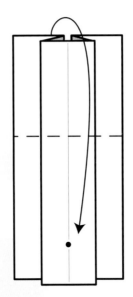

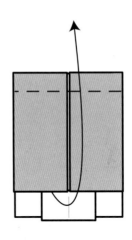

5 Turn over and rotate the paper to a vertical position.

6 Fold the top edge down to a little above the bottom edge.

7 Fold the same edge back up again, forming a pleat at the 'waistline'.

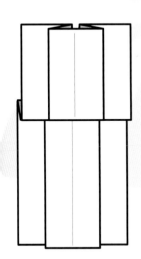

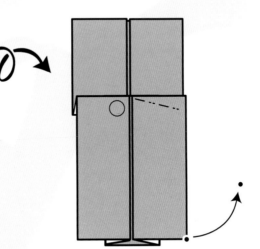

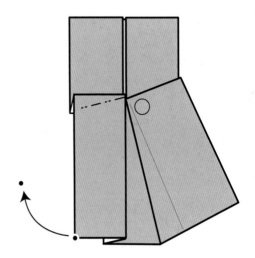

8 Turn over, side to side.

9 Hold the model at the circle. Grasp the bottom right corner and swing it to the right and up, as far as it will comfortably go.

10 Flatten the skirt section in this new position. Repeat step 9 on the left.

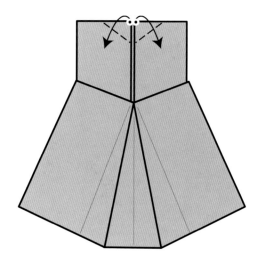

11 Fold down the top middle corners to determine how deep or shallow the V-neckline is to be.

12 Crease extra sharply and unfold. Turn over to the back of the dress.

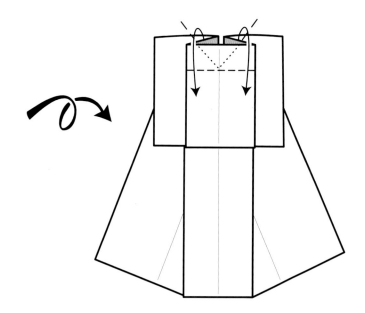

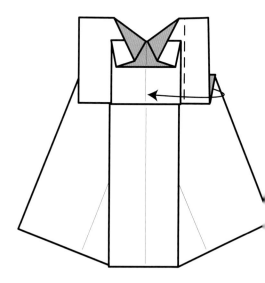

13 Grasp the two top corners of the inner edges. Fold down the top of the mid-section, using the bottom of the V-neckline as a guide. Step 14 shows the result.

14 Lift the waistline corner and fold the right side panel inwards.

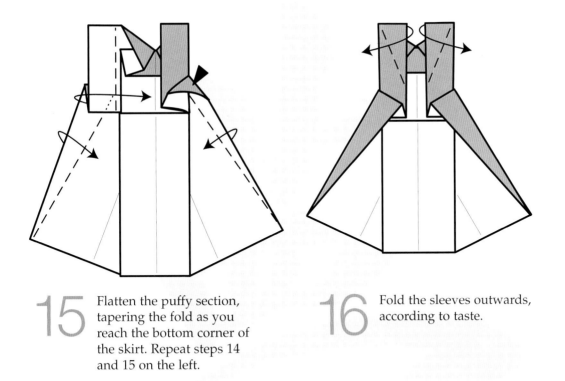

15 Flatten the puffy section, tapering the fold as you reach the bottom corner of the skirt. Repeat steps 14 and 15 on the left.

16 Fold the sleeves outwards, according to taste.

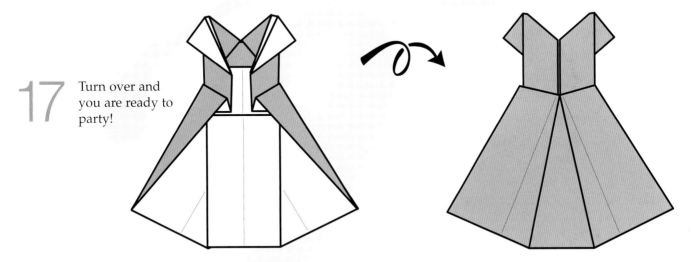

17 Turn over and you are ready to party!

18 The height of the bodice, depth of the neckline, and size of the sleeves can all be varied by adjusting the folds in steps 6, 7, 11 and 16.

Origin: The Party Dress is a modification of a jumpsuit model by Hyun Sook Go. The creator Alison Reisel found a diagram for the Jumpsuit in a package of Korean origami paper.

Two-tone dress

This casual dress is a variation on Alison Reisel's Party Dress. Use duo paper with a coordinating colour or pattern on the reverse side.

Card design by Sok Song.

Level: Intermediate.

Paper: A square measuring approximately 13cm (5in).

Creator: Alison Reisel and Mary Ellen Palmeri (USA).

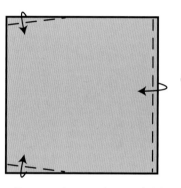

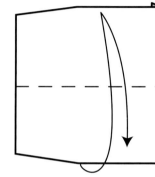

1 Dress colour side up, fold in narrow hems for the cuffs on the sleeves and trim on the bottom of the skirt.

2 Turn over to the trim colour side, and proceed as for the Party Dress, steps 1 to 5.

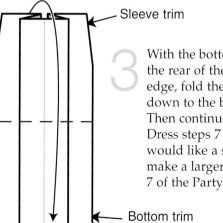

Sleeve trim

Bottom trim

3 With the bottom trim at the rear of the bottom edge, fold the top edge down to the bottom edge. Then continue with Party Dress steps 7 to 10. If you would like a short bodice, make a larger pleat at step 7 of the Party Dress.

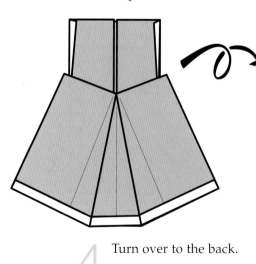

4 Turn over to the back.

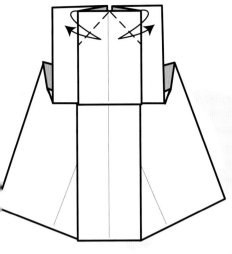

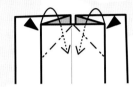

5 Fold the inner top corners to the centre-line. Crease sharply and unfold.

6 Inside-reverse-fold the creases just made.

7 Lower the loose point.

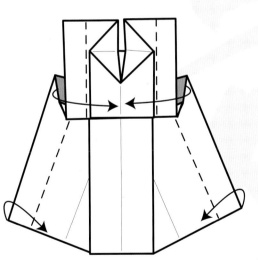

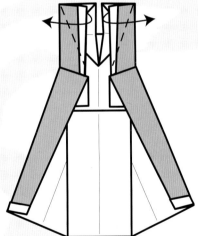

8 Fold in the sides of the bodice and skirt. Instead of tapering the skirt to the bottom corner, fold in a little more, as shown.

9 Fold the corners outward to form the sleeves. Then turn over to the front.

10 Fold down a collar, according to taste.

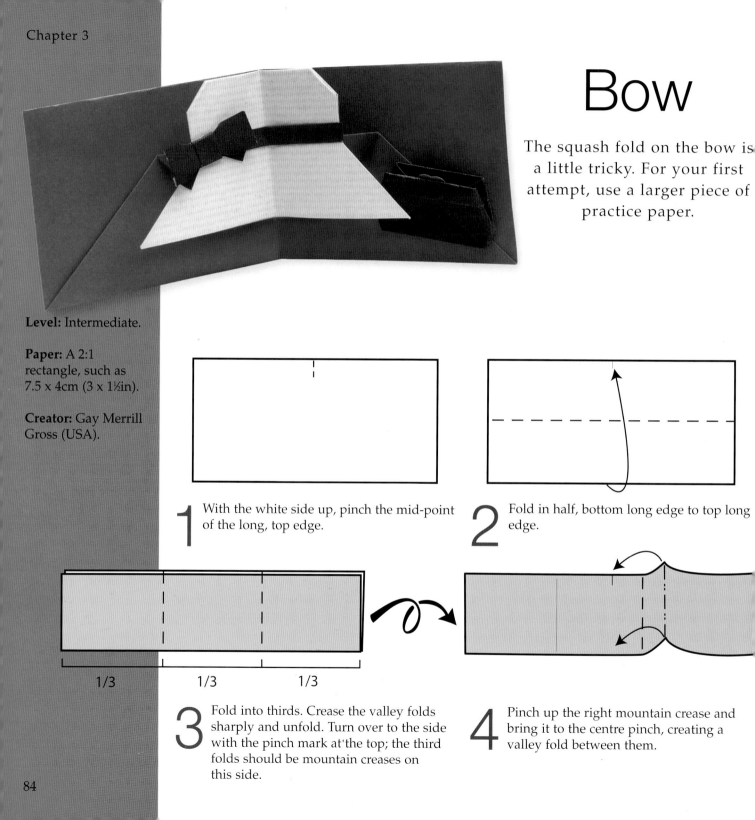

Bow

The squash fold on the bow is a little tricky. For your first attempt, use a larger piece of practice paper.

Level: Intermediate.

Paper: A 2:1 rectangle, such as 7.5 x 4cm (3 x 1½in).

Creator: Gay Merrill Gross (USA).

1 With the white side up, pinch the mid-point of the long, top edge.

2 Fold in half, bottom long edge to top long edge.

1/3   1/3   1/3

3 Fold into thirds. Crease the valley folds sharply and unfold. Turn over to the side with the pinch mark at the top; the third folds should be mountain creases on this side.

4 Pinch up the right mountain crease and bring it to the centre pinch, creating a valley fold between them.

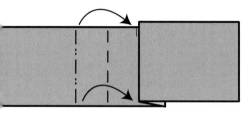

5 Repeat step 4 on the left.

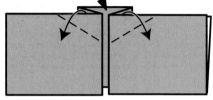

6 One at a time, pull down (at an angle) a bit of the top edge next to the inner corners. Then press on the puffy section that was the inner corner, forming a squash fold as shown in drawing 7.

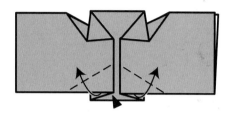

7 Repeat step 6 on the bottom.

8 Lower the centre top edge as far as possible. The squash folds should also shift slightly downwards. Repeat at the bottom.

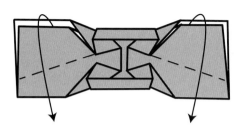

9 At the top right corner, separate the front and rear layers. Pull the front layer down to the position shown in drawing 10. As you do this, the section under the squash fold will loosen and lower too. Repeat on the left.

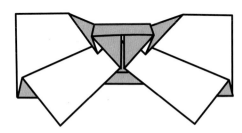

10 Turn the Bow over.

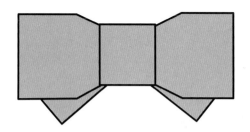

11 The Bow can be used as a decoration on the Hat, (page 76) Ribboned Present (page 7) or one of the Dress models (pages 78 and 82).

modular decorations

Modular origami, also known as unit origami, is a clever way of joining folded units, or modules, to create multi-piece creations. Just as LEGO® pieces are joined together by means of pegs and sockets, origami units can be similarly constructed with points and pockets. The point on each unit fits snugly into the pocket of its neighbouring unit, thus locking the units together and allowing the formation of multi-piece constructions requiring no glue.

Modulars consist of two or more units, depending on the design. Some three-dimensional modulars use 30, 90, or even hundreds of units. With flat, two-dimensional modulars, a beautiful kaleidoscopic effect can be achieved by folding units from identically patterned papers.

Rosette

The overlapping layers of the Rosette make a very three-dimensional model – a great effect on a card.

Level: Low Intermediate.

Paper: Eight small squares, each approximately 5–7.5cm (2–3in). Identically patterned papers will give a kaleidoscopic effect.

Creator: Darren Scott (Australia).

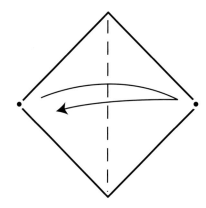

1 White side up, fold in half, corner to corner. Crease and unfold.

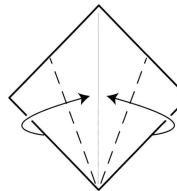

2 Fold the two lower edges inwards to meet at the centre, forming an ice cream cone shape.

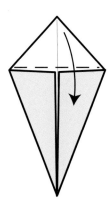

3 Bring the ice cream triangle down, folding along the top edge of the cone.

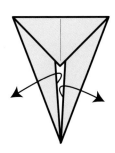

4 Unfold the right and left cone flaps, leaving the ice cream triangle in place.

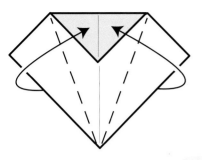

5 Fold the cone flaps inwards again, covering the ice cream triangle.

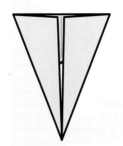

6 The cone is restored but the ice cream triangle is hidden inside. Turn over to the non-split side of the cone.

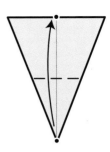
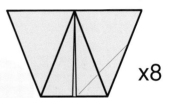

7 Fold the bottom corner up to the mid-point of the top edge.

8 Fold the right half of the bottom edge to the centre, leaving a very slight gap.

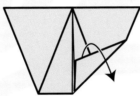

9 Crease sharply and unfold. This pre-crease will make it easier to lock the units together.

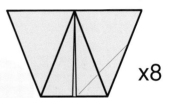

x8

10 The Rosette unit is complete. Now fold another seven units‹

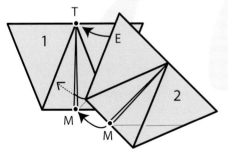

11 Insert the left bottom corner of unit 2 into the left pocket of unit 1. Mid-points 'M' will touch each other, and edge 'E' will touch top point 'T'.

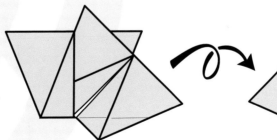

12 Check to make sure the units are aligned as shown in the drawing. Holding them securely in place, turn over to perform the lock.

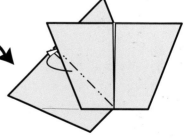

13 On the front unit, refold along the existing mountain crease, wrapping this small triangular flap around the cut edge of the rear unit, locking the two together.

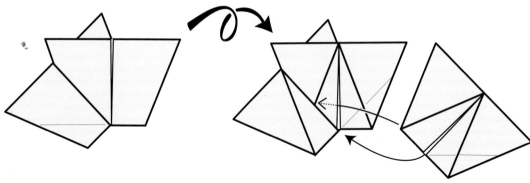

14 The two units are now locked together. Turn back to the front.

15 Continue joining units on the right, following steps 11 to 14. After connecting unit 8 to unit 7, bring unit 1 to the front and connect it to unit 8, completing the circle.

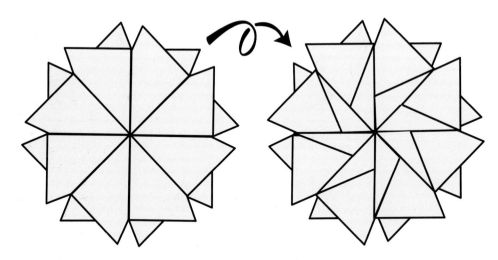

16 The finished Rosette looks attractive from the back . . .

. . and the front. The model can be used as an ornament by attaching a decorative thread.

You can also use the model as a reversible pin. Insert a tie tack or lapel pinback through the hole in the centre.

Florette

The Florette is a variation of the Rosette on
page 88. The 'ice cream' triangle is left out instead
of folding it into the cone. This makes larger 'petals'
and shows off a border or other design on an
outside corner of the paper.

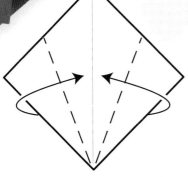

Level: Low
intermediate.

Paper: Eight small
squares, each
approximately
5–7.5cm (2–3in).
Identically
patterned papers
will give a
kaleidoscopic effect.

Creator: Darren
Scott (Australia).

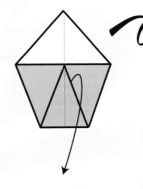
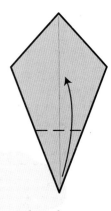

1 Follow steps 1 and 2 for
the Rosette (page 88),
forming an ice cream
cone.

2 Fold the bottom
corner to the
mid-point of the
top edge of the
cone.

3 Crease
sharply and
unfold.
Turn over
to . . .

4 . . . the other
side. Smooth the
horizontal crease
flat to erase the
bump from the
mountain crease,
then change the
crease to a
valley fold.

5 Now follow steps 8 to 15
for the Rosette.

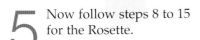

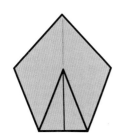

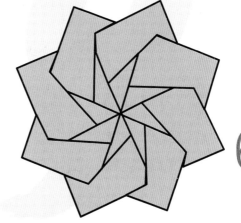

6 The finished
Florette makes a
great package
decoration.

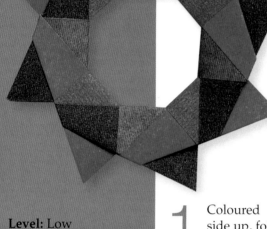

Star wreath

This Star Wreath offers many possibilities
for creative use. To make a card decoration or ornament
use 4–5cm (1½–2in) squares. To make a beautiful wreath use
6–9cm (2½–3½in) squares.

Level: Low
Intermediate.

Paper: Eight squares
of either duo or
mono-coloured
paper. Origami
paper, memo cube
paper, or foil
giftwrap, are all good
choices.

Creator: Courtney
Spooner Clark
(USA).

1 Coloured side up, fold in half, top edge to bottom edge.

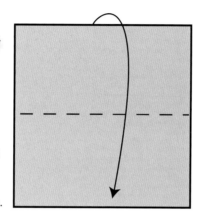

2 Fold the bottom right corner, front layer only, up to top folded edge.

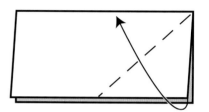

3 Unfold the triangular flap.

4 Raise the bottom right corner again, aligning the crease just made with the top folded edge (see drawing 5).

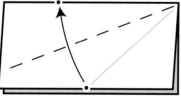

5 Turn over, side to side.

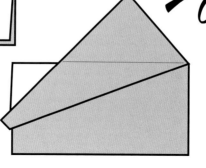

6 Raise the bottom left corner up to lie exactly over the top right corner.

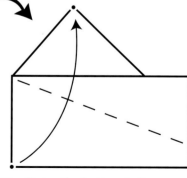

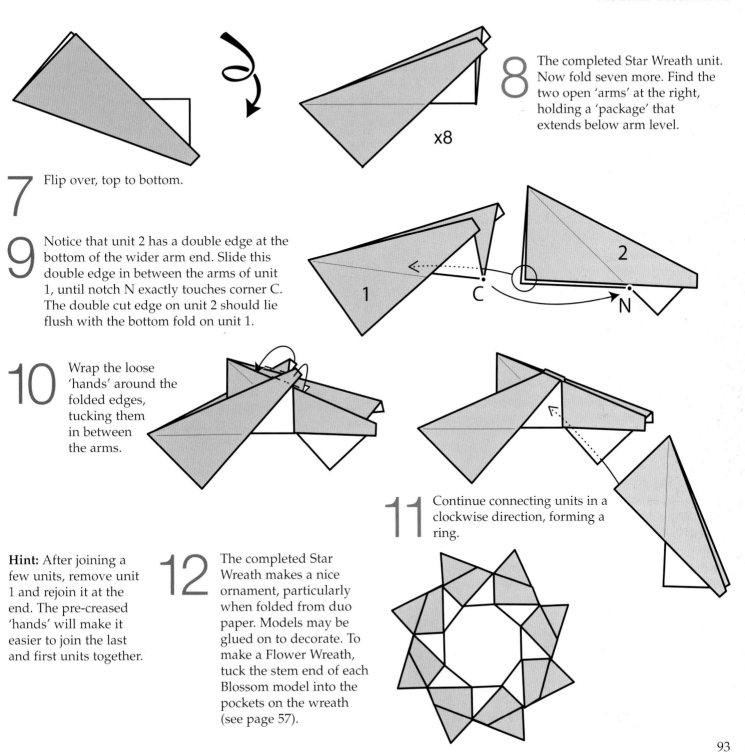

8 The completed Star Wreath unit. Now fold seven more. Find the two open 'arms' at the right, holding a 'package' that extends below arm level.

x8

7 Flip over, top to bottom.

9 Notice that unit 2 has a double edge at the bottom of the wider arm end. Slide this double edge in between the arms of unit 1, until notch N exactly touches corner C. The double cut edge on unit 2 should lie flush with the bottom fold on unit 1.

10 Wrap the loose 'hands' around the folded edges, tucking them in between the arms.

11 Continue connecting units in a clockwise direction, forming a ring.

Hint: After joining a few units, remove unit 1 and rejoin it at the end. The pre-creased 'hands' will make it easier to join the last and first units together.

12 The completed Star Wreath makes a nice ornament, particularly when folded from duo paper. Models may be glued on to decorate. To make a Flower Wreath, tuck the stem end of each Blossom model into the pockets on the wreath (see page 57).

Eight-point star

This model actually has both an inner and an outer eight-point star. It looks lovely made in shaded or patterned paper.

Level: Low Intermediate.

Paper: Eight squares.

Creator: Ildikó H. Vass (Hungary).

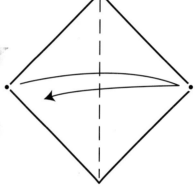

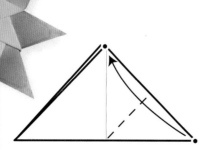

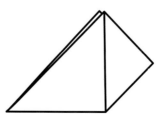

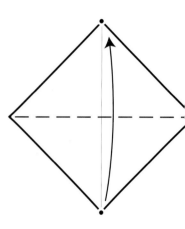

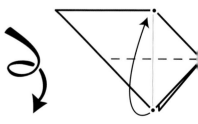

1 White side up, fold in half, side corner to side corner. Crease sharply and unfold.

2 Fold in half, bottom corner to top corner, forming a coloured triangle.

3 Fold the right arm up to the top corner.

4 Flip the paper over, top to bottom.

5 Fold the double-layered bottom corner up to the top, leaving behind the arm corner.

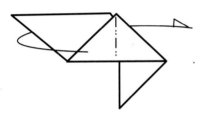

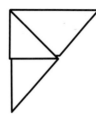

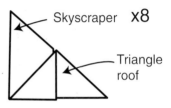

Skyscraper ×8

Triangle roof

6 Mountain-fold along the centre crease, bringing the left part of the model behind the right part.

7 Rotate the paper slightly anti-clockwise, giving . . .

8 . . . a triangular roof flap in front of a skyscraper flap. (The Citicorp Building in New York City has a slanted roof like the rear flap.) This is the finished unit. Fold seven more units.

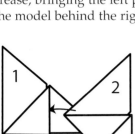

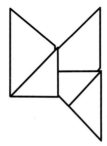

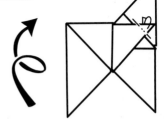

9 Hold unit 2 so that it looks like an arrowhead pointing left to the pocket on unit 1. Insert the right-angled corner on unit 2 into the pocket on unit 1, fitting it in as far as possible.

10 Holding the two units tightly together, flip them over, bottom to top.

11 On the back, wrap the tip of the loose point around the folded edge, as snugly as possible, locking the two units together.

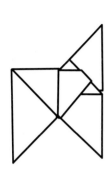

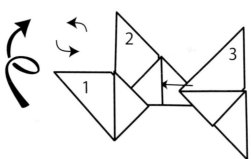

12 Flip over again, bottom to top.

13 On the front, insert the right angle corner on unit 3 into the pocket on unit 2, then turn over to the back and lock them together, repeating step 11. Continue in this manner, connecting all eight units.

14 The finished Eight-Point Star is attractive from both the front and the back. It makes a beautiful card decoration, or it can be hung as an ornament.

Six-point star

This six-point modular star is made from just two sheets of paper.
It can be attached to a card or used as a hanging decoration.

Level: Intermediate.

Paper: Two equilateral triangles (see page 16); each can be a different colour. The finished star will be two-thirds the height of the starting triangles. For example, a triangle that is 15cm (6in) high will make a 10cm (4in) star.

Creator: Lewis Simon (USA).

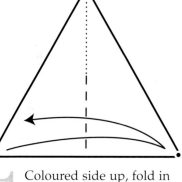

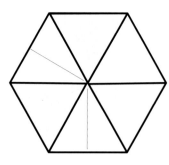

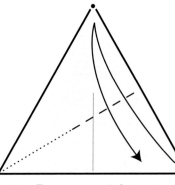

1 Coloured side up, fold in half, corner to corner, but crease only from the centre down to the edge. Avoid creasing the corner.

2 Repeat step 1, bringing together two other corners. The intersection of the two creases will locate the centre of the triangle.

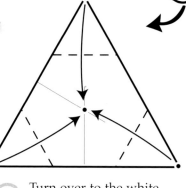

3 Turn over to the white side. Fold all three corners inwards to meet at the centre-point.

4 Turn over, side to side, so that a cut edge remains at the bottom.

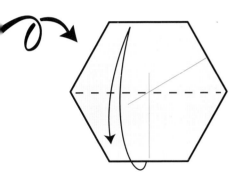

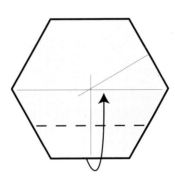

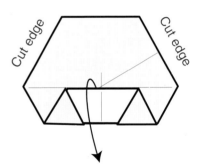

5 Fold the bottom cut edge up to the top folded edge. The fold will connect two corners. Crease and unfold.

6 Make sure the bottom edge is still a cut edge and fold it to the centre.

7 Unfold the cut-edge flap and repeat steps 5 to 7 two more times, always with a cut edge at the bottom. Leave the last flap in place.

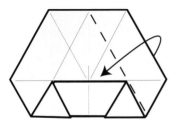

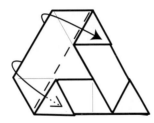

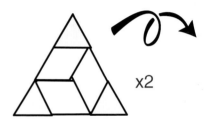

8 Fold the right cut edge to the centre on the existing crease.

9 Fold the left cut edge to the centre, tucking it under the lower flap.

10 Turn over to the front and the unit is complete. Fold a second unit.

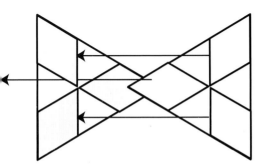

11 To join the two units together, position them so that two corners overlap. Slide the leading corner of the front unit under two diamond-shaped flaps of the rear unit until the flaps are aligned as in drawing 12.

12 Gently flex the far right corner backwards until the hidden corner flips forwards. Wrap it around the white edge and align it with the other centre corners.

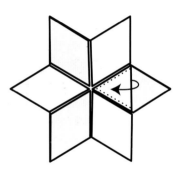

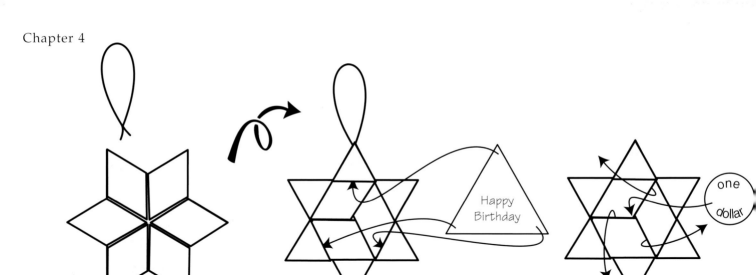

13 The Six-Point Star can be attached to a card or a gift tag. You may also hang it as an ornament. At step 9, insert the knot end of a loop of metallic thread under a flap before folding over the last flap.

14 Make the star into a hanging greeting. Turn the star over to the back. Cut an equilateral triangle from medium-weight paper, a little smaller than one of the finished units from step 10. Insert the triangle into the pockets on the back of the star.

In the Jewish tradition, children are given coins, or gelt, on the holiday of Chanukah. If you unfold the rear flaps of the 6-Point Star you can insert a coin and then reclose. Folder Paul Weinberg encloses the gelt for his grandchildren and calls this a 'Gelt Giver'.

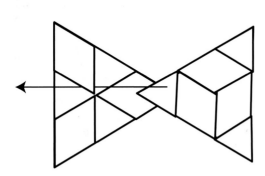

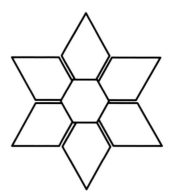

15 To make a three-coloured star cut the original equilateral triangles from different coloured duo papers and carry out steps 1–10. Before joining at step 11, turn one unit over and then join as before. Three colours will show on both sides of the finished star.

16 **Challenge:** Here are some variations I created on Lewis Simon's 6-Point Star. See if you can work them out from the drawings. If you fold the first from tracing paper and hold it up to the light, look for the hidden inner star pattern! Experiment with the model to discover other variations, some may work well as frames.

Button flower

The Button Flower makes a colourful corner clip or a decoration for a card or letterfold. This modular is made from a leaf unit that wraps around a flower unit.

Outer Petals

Inner Petals

Leaf Unit

Level: Low Intermediate.

Paper: Two small squares of equal size, such as 4cm (½in), one for the leaf, one for the outer petals of the flower. For the inner petals use one square two-thirds that of the larger squares, such as 2.5cm (1in). Use paper that is coloured on both sides.

Creator: Gay Merrill Gross (USA)..

**FLOWER UNIT –
Outer petals**

Use one of the larger squares.

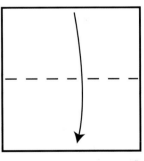

1 With the white side up, fold in half, top edge to bottom edge.

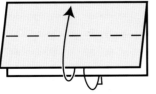

2 Fold the bottom cut edge of the front layer up to the top folded edge. Turn over and repeat behind.

3 Completely unfold the paper as shown, and rotate it so the creases just made are vertical.

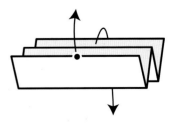

99

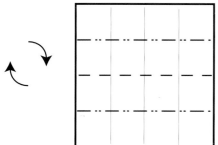

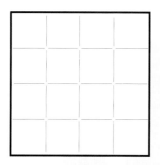

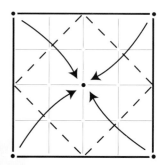

4 White side up (the existing centre crease should be a valley crease), repeat steps 1 to 3 in the direction shown.

5 The paper is now divided into a grid of 16 small squares.

6 White side still up (centre creases are valleys), fold the four outer corners to the centre. In origami, this is called a blintz fold.

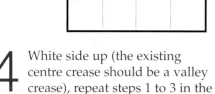

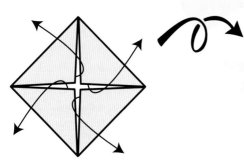

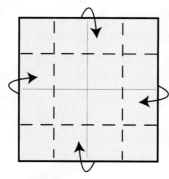

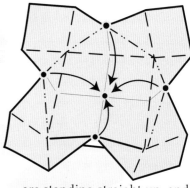

7 Unfold the paper and turn over to the coloured side where the quarter-creases are valley.

8 Begin to refold on the existing quarter-creases until the sides . . .

9 . . . are standing straight up, and the paper resembles an angular dish. Bring the mid-point of each edge inwards and down to the centre of the square, collapsing along the existing creases.

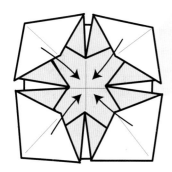

10 Press the paper flat, giving four small squares on the near surface of the paper. This forms an origami base called a Froebel Pattern Fold.

11 Take each loose corner from the middle and fold it outwards to lie over an outer corner.

12 The completed outer petals. This is one of the many traditional patterns that can be created by adding folds to the flaps of the Froebel Pattern Fold.

FLOWER UNIT Inner petals

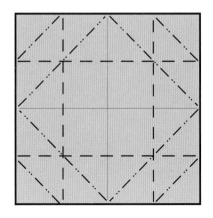

1 Using the smaller square, follow instructions 1 to 11 for the outer petals.

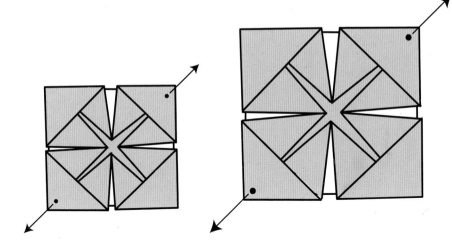

2 Grasp two opposite loose corners and spread them apart until you have a half-open form. Repeat on the outer petals.

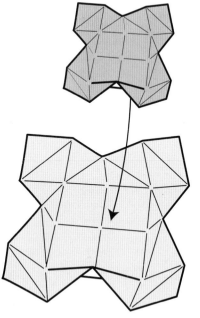

3 Nest the smaller flower into the larger and interlock the two.

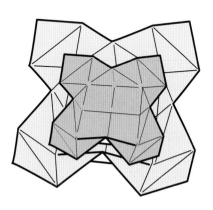

4 Re-flatten the two petal units. As you do so, make sure the tips of the inner petals remain on the outside and do not hide under the outer petals.

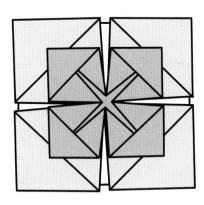

5 The completed flower unit.

101

Chapter 4

LEAF UNIT Use the other large square the same size as the square you used for the outer petals.

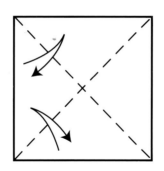

1 White side up, fold diagonally in half and unfold. Repeat in the other direction.

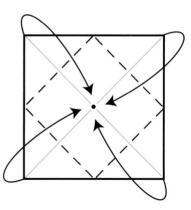

2 Blintz-fold all four corners to the centre (see step 6 for outer petals).

3 Turn over to the side without flaps.

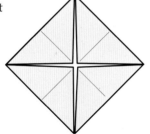

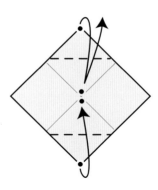

4 Fold the top and bottom corners almost to the centre, leaving a small gap between the two. Unfold the top flap but leave the lower flap in place.

5 Turn over to the back.

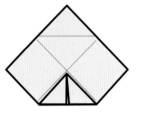

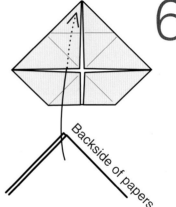

Backside of papers

6 The leaf is complete. Slide the back side of the corner or corners you wish to decorate or fasten together, into the horizontal slit on the leaf unit. Push the corners upward as far as they will go.

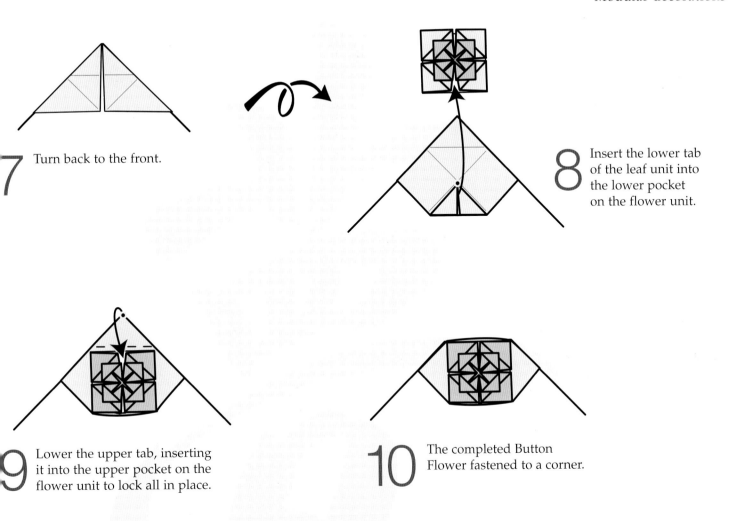

7 Turn back to the front.

8 Insert the lower tab of the leaf unit into the lower pocket on the flower unit.

9 Lower the upper tab, inserting it into the upper pocket on the flower unit to lock all in place.

10 The completed Button Flower fastened to a corner.

Origin: The Froebel Pattern Fold is named after German educator, Friedrich Froebel. In the 1800s he founded the kindergarten, based on his ideas that children can learn through manipulation of materials and structured play. One of the many 'hands-on' activities he encouraged was paperfolding. This pattern fold in particular, offers a starting point from which many decorative, flower-like designs can be discovered, allowing the folder to experiment and be creative. (See page 38 for another example).

Flower unit

Inner petals

Leaf unit

Level: Intermediate.

Paper: Four squares of equal size, each approximately 6cm (2½in) square, for the leaf units and the outer petals of the flower units. Two smaller squares approximately 4cm (1½in) big for the inner petals.

Makers: Gay Merrill Gross and Deanna Kwan (USA).

Button flower ornament

Two Button Flowers joined back to back, form this decorative ornament. Tuck it inside your correspondence as an extra surprise.

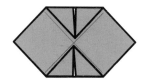

x2   x2

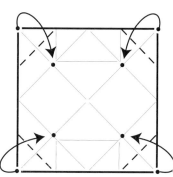

1 Following the instructions for the Button Flower on pages 99–103, fold two leaf units and two flower units. Completely unfold only one leaf unit.

2 With the white side up, fold each outer corner of the unfolded leaf unit to the nearest intersection of creases.

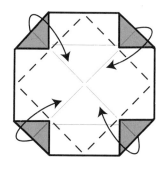

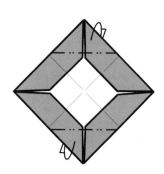

3 Refold on the existing slanted creases, forming a 'picture frame.'

4 Turn over and replace the triangular locking tabs.

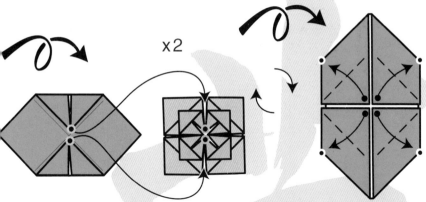

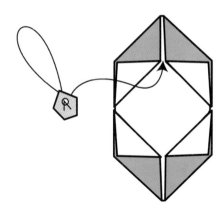

5 Join together both sets of flower and leaf units.

6 On the back of the second leaf unit, fold each inner, loose corner outwards to an outer corner, forming four triangular tabs.

7 Thread a loop of metallic thread through a pinprick in a scrap of paper and tie a knot. Slide the scrap into the top slit on the leaf unit.

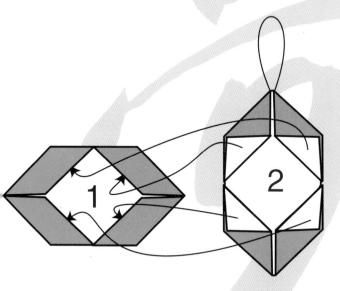

8 Hold one Button Flower horizontally, the other vertically. Insert each triangular tab from leaf unit 2 into a pocket on leaf unit 1, joining the two together. If it's easier for you, temporarily remove the flower unit and partially unfold leaf unit 1.

9 The finished ornament has a Button Flower on both the front and back.

tatos and
paper pockets

Tato is a Japanese word for a self-closing paper pouch. Traditionally these were used to hold small household items such as thread, buttons or stamps.

Many of these models have a wonderful spring action – when you tug on their flaps they stretch open and then spring back to a closed position.

These clever containers can be used to enclose an elegant invitation or good wishes. Alternatively, they can be filled with a fun collection of flat origami to wish the recipient a year filled with many wonderful things.

Layered pocket

These pockets can be attached to a card or left loose as a 'tuck-in' inside an envelope or letter. Use them to hold a message card or a small memento on a scrapbook page.

Level: Simple.

Paper: Two or three squares in graduated sizes and different colours. Your largest square should be coloured on both sides.

Creator: Traditional.

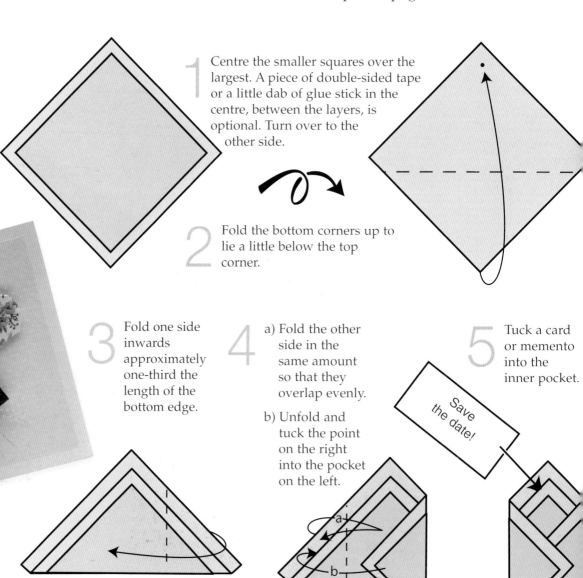

1 Centre the smaller squares over the largest. A piece of double-sided tape or a little dab of glue stick in the centre, between the layers, is optional. Turn over to the other side.

2 Fold the bottom corners up to lie a little below the top corner.

3 Fold one side inwards approximately one-third the length of the bottom edge.

4 a) Fold the other side in the same amount so that they overlap evenly.

b) Unfold and tuck the point on the right into the pocket on the left.

5 Tuck a card or memento into the inner pocket.

Save the date!

Surprise Package

A slight tug on the flaps transforms this flat package into a three-dimensional box. Use it to enclose a special message or invitation or fill it with origami surprises, photos, or other small treasures.

Level: Intermediate.

Paper: A rectangle such as A4 will work well (see the note on page 111). Duo paper (a different colour or pattern on each side) is very effective.

Creator: Gay Merrill Gross (USA).

Origin: Variation on a traditional design.

1 White side up, divide the long edges into equal thirds (see page 15). Leave a single fold in place.

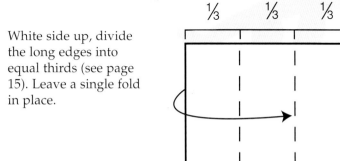

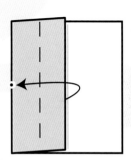

2 Fold the flap in half.

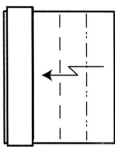

3 Repeat steps 1 and 2 on the right: refold on the third fold and then fold the new flap in half.

109

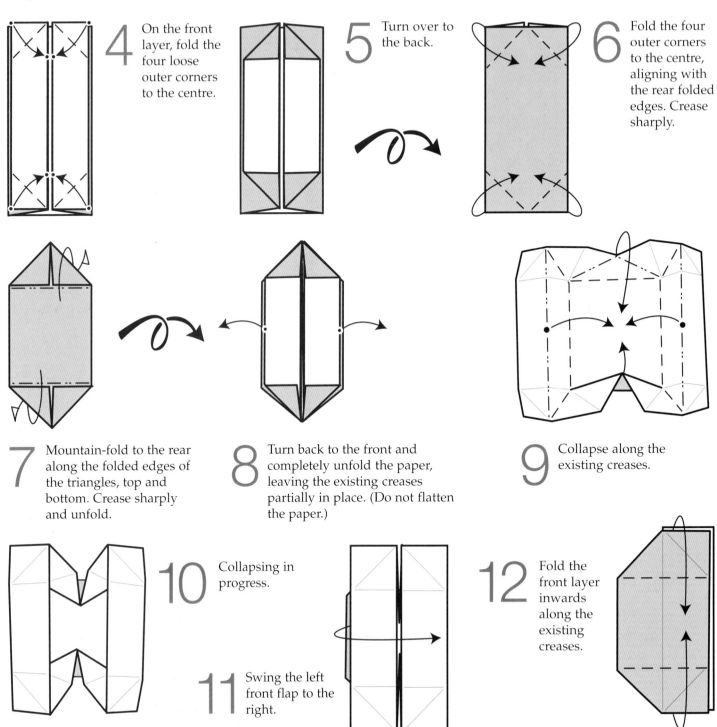

4 On the front layer, fold the four loose outer corners to the centre.

5 Turn over to the back.

6 Fold the four outer corners to the centre, aligning with the rear folded edges. Crease sharply.

7 Mountain-fold to the rear along the folded edges of the triangles, top and bottom. Crease sharply and unfold.

8 Turn back to the front and completely unfold the paper, leaving the existing creases partially in place. (Do not flatten the paper.)

9 Collapse along the existing creases.

10 Collapsing in progress.

11 Swing the left front flap to the right.

12 Fold the front layer inwards along the existing creases.

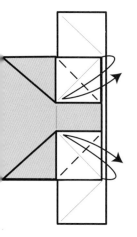

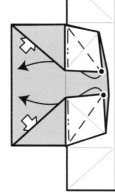

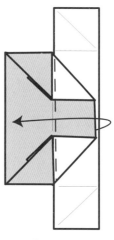

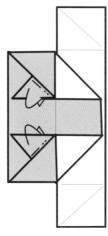

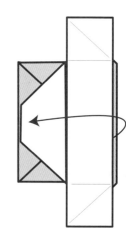

13
Fold the loose corners to the opposite corner. Crease sharply and partially unfold, creating a diagonal crease on the two small squares.

14
Slightly lift the slanted folded edges of the triangles on the left. Then drag the inner right-angled corners to the left and behind the triangles.

15
Mountain-fold the loose triangular tabs under the larger triangles.

16
Flip the front right flap to the left.

17
Repeat steps 11 to 16 on the right.

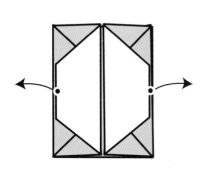

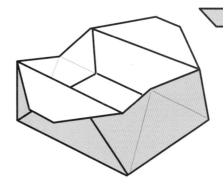

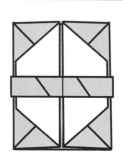

18
Pull the flaps away from each other and the box will open.

19
The finished Surprise Package is ready to fill with good wishes, mementos, or fun treats.

20
A ribbon or paper band can be used to keep the package closed.

Note If you start with a 1:1.5 rectangle, the finished model will be square. This is a traditional design except for the lock (steps 14 and 15).

Level: Simple.

Paper: A rectangle twice the width of the finished stand, and eight times the height. To learn the model, use a sheet of A4 paper.

Creator: Gay Merrill Gross (USA).

Standing pocket

Slide an origami model or note into the pocket and leave it sitting on the kitchen table or desk as an early morning surprise. This model can also be used for a pop-up greeting or a place card.

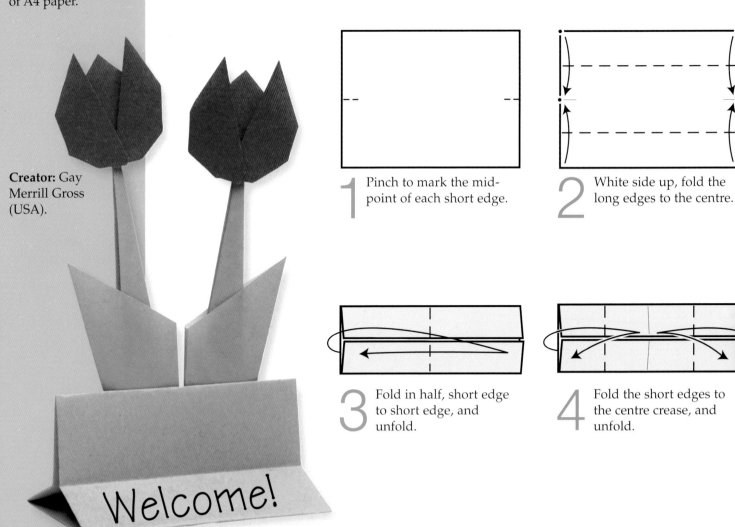

1 Pinch to mark the mid-point of each short edge.

2 White side up, fold the long edges to the centre.

3 Fold in half, short edge to short edge, and unfold.

4 Fold the short edges to the centre crease, and unfold.

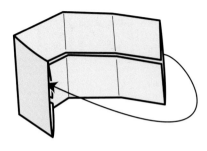

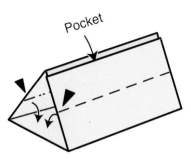

Pocket

5 Insert one short edge into the other until the cut edges reach the first quarter-crease, forming a triangular prism.

6 Sit the model on the table so that the pocket edge is on top. Pinch the top edge with both hands and inch your fingers down to the table, giving the Standing Pocket shown in drawing 7. Reinforce the creases just created by folding the pocket flap towards you and away from you, and then stand it up straight.

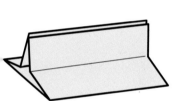

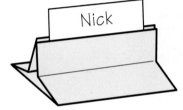

Nick

7 Insert a card or origami model into the Standing Pocket.

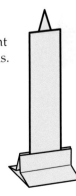

Variations:
Experiment with rectangles of different sizes and proportions.

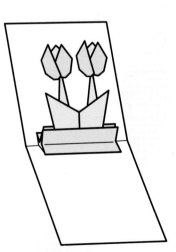

Make a pop-up card!

A candle Standing Pocket makes a perfect Christmas table decoration.

113

Pleated Triangle

This model has a striking geometric pattern.
The narrowing folds require neat, very tiny folds.

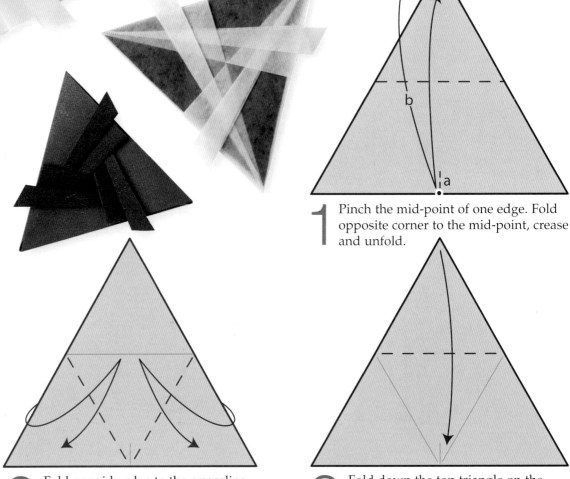

Level: Intermediate.

Paper: An equilateral triangle (see page 16). Duo paper (a different colour on each side) is recommended.

Creator: Susana Arashiro (Argentina).

1 Pinch the mid-point of one edge. Fold opposite corner to the mid-point, crease and unfold.

2 Fold one side edge to the creaseline and unfold. Repeat with the other side edge.

3 Fold down the top triangle on the existing crease.

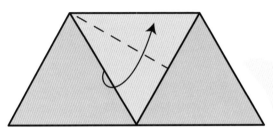

4 Fold the left edge of the triangular flap to the top folded edge.

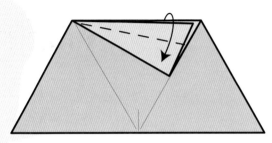

5 Fold the cut edge to the folded edge, creating a very slender triangular flap.

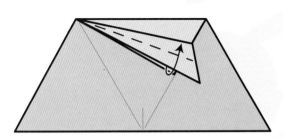

6 Fold the same cut edge to the new folded edge, narrowing the slender triangle one more time.

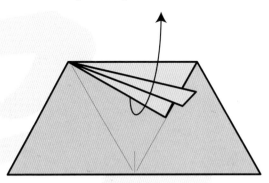

7 This completes the pleating on one flap. Lift the flap out of the way and repeat steps 3 to 7 on the other two flaps.

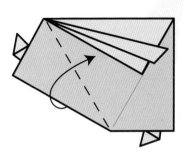

8 Refold the left flap inwards, covering the tail end of the top pleats.

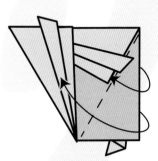

9 Fold the right flap inwards, inserting its tail end under the top flap.

10 The Pleated Triangle makes a unique holder for a message, a pretty leaf or a pressed flower. If you fold it from vellum or tracing paper you will be able to see through to the contents.

115

Pinwheel tato and toy

This decorative paper pouch twists open and closed, very much like a Moroccan purse. Use it to enclose good wishes, a souvenir on a scrapbook page, or a small gift.

This version of a traditional *tato* comes from *Origami Feest*, by Dutch folder Everdien Tigelaar.

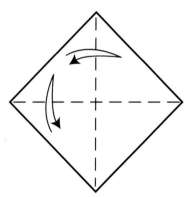

Level: Intermediate.

Paper: Two squares of equal size; each can be a different colour.

Creator: Traditional.

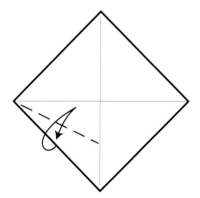

1 White side up, fold the square diagonally in half and unfold. Repeat in the other direction.

2 Fold the bottom left edge to the horizontal centre-line. Crease only from the side corner to the vertical centre-line and unfold.

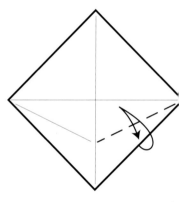

3 Repeat step 2 on the right.

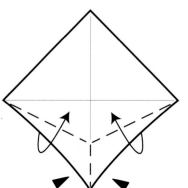

4 Make a rabbit-ear fold. As you pinch the bottom corner in half, refold on the existing creases, bringing the lower edges upwards to the horizontal centre-line.

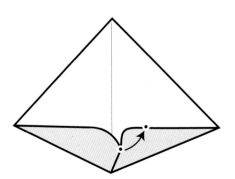

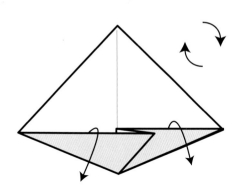

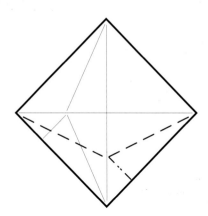

5 Push the point (the rabbit ear) to the right and flatten.

6 The completed rabbit ear. Unfold the paper and rotate 90°.

7 Repeat steps 2 to 6 on the new bottom corner and then the other two corners. Always flatten the rabbit ear to the right.

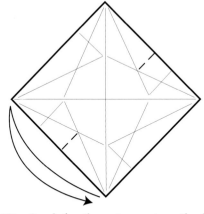

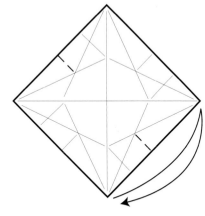

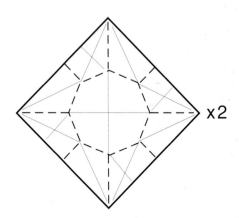

8 Look for the octagon inscribed within the square. Fold the square in half, edge to edge, creasing only in the sections outside the octagon. Unfold.

9 Repeat in the other direction.

10 Reinforce the valley creases shown – the inner octagon and the creases that radiate from the octagon's corners. The paper should start to shape into a shallow bowl form. Repeat steps 1 to 10 on the second square.

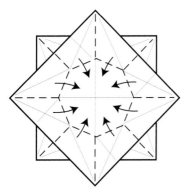

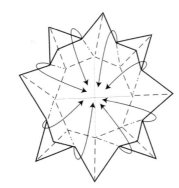

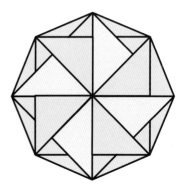

11 Lay the second square over the first as shown. Pinch the outer points in half, then push them inwards and down towards the centre of the octagon.

12 Step 11 in progress. When all of the points are fully pinched in half, begin flattening each to the right in an anti-clockwise direction.

13 The finished Pinwheel Tato. Open it, place a special wish or a surprise inside, then collapse it to close.

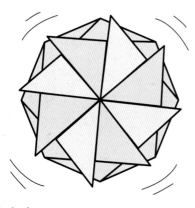

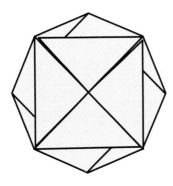

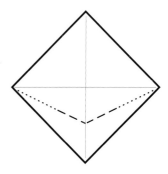

Variation
To make a spinning top, make the Pinwheel Tato from two small squares 9cm (3½in) or smaller. Let the pinwheel points stand up a little. Place the model on a flat, smooth surface and blow gently over the centre of it. If the model doesn't spin well, go back to step 1 and sharpen the diagonal folds.

You can also make a spinning top by collapsing a single sheet folded as for steps 1–10. Try adding folds to the loose flaps to form decorative designs.

If you are an experienced folder, you can make steps 2 and 3 partial creases, sharpening only the sections shown. This will eliminate extra creases on the finished model. Repeat on all four corners.

Origin: The single sheet version of this model is included in Isao Honda's 1964 book, *Noshi – Classic Origami in Japan*. Honda explains that this octagonal case is thought to represent *Yata no Kagami*, the Sacred Mirror, one of three sacred Imperial treasures. *Yata no Kagami* is a symbol of the Supreme Shinto deity, the Sun Goddess Amaterasu Omikami, who blesses all with supreme light.

Flower tato

Level: Challenging.

Paper: Four squares in four different colours. Cut each square in half along the diagonal to give you eight right-angled triangles.

Creator: Yoshihide Momotani (Japan).

BLOSSOM VERSION

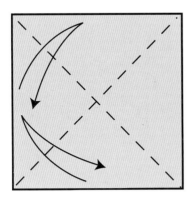

1 Inner-colour side up, fold and unfold along both diagonals. Turn over to the outer-colour side.

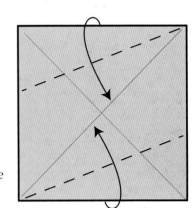

2 Fold the lower edge inwards to the diagonal crease. Fold the top edge to the same diagonal.

3 You now have two half ice cream cone folds. Turn over to the side without flaps.

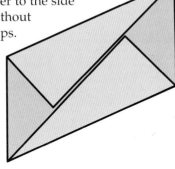

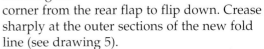

4 Bring the bottom folded edge up to the top folded edge, allowing the corner from the rear flap to flip down. Crease sharply at the outer sections of the new fold line (see drawing 5).

5 After creasing sharply where shown, unfold the paper, outer-colour side up, and reposition the paper with the new creases slanting from bottom to top.

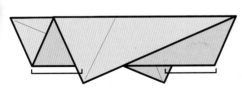

6 Repeat steps 2 to 4 with the new top and bottom edges.

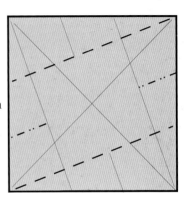

7 Open the paper to the inner-colour side. Notice the slanted partial folds at the top and bottom would connect through the centre of the square, if the creases were extended. Fold endpoint E to intersection I, and corner C to creaseline L.

Crease sharply between the two inner intersection points indicated in the drawing.

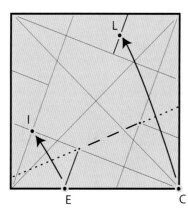

8 Make a sharp partial fold where shown. Unfold back to a square and rotate the paper by 90°.

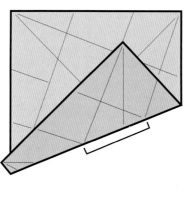

9 Repeat steps 7 and 8 with the new bottom edge and then the other two edges.

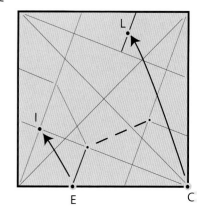

10 The creases just made inscribe an inner square. Reinforce the inner-square creases and the creases shown that extend from the corners of that square, forming an angular bowl shape.

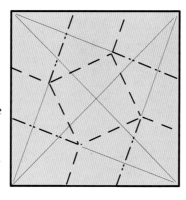

11 As you pinch two opposite sides where shown, twist your left hand away from you and your right hand towards you, collapsing the paper in an anti-clockwise direction, into the flat Flower Tato.

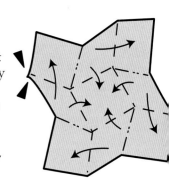

12 The finished Flower Tato – blossom version. Gently pulling two opposite petals apart will open the tato so you can insert a message or folded treat.

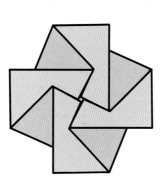

FOLDING TIP:

After you have folded the model several times you can avoid extra creases in the model by creasing sharply only where shown.

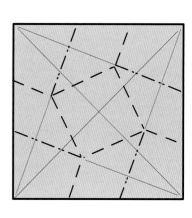

Flower tato

From the same crease pattern as the blossom version, Yoshihide Momotani has created a different 'star' design. As you spread the petals of these magical flower forms, the base will twist to reveal a hidden message.

Level: Challenging.

Paper: A square, any size. Both sides of the paper will show on the finished tato.

Creator: Yoshihide Momotani (Japan).

Origin: Yoshihide Momotani created these two Flower tato versions by modifying a twist-fold wrapping from the classic Japanese tradition. They appear in his 1993 book *Wrapping Origami*.

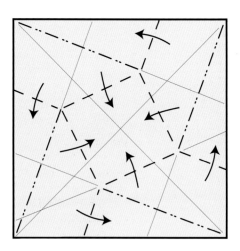

STAR VERSION

1 Open the Flower Tato – Blossom version. Reinforce the creases shown. Collapse in an anti-clockwise direction for the . . .

2 Flower Tato – Star version. This form can be used in a variety of ways, such as an ornament or gift tag. Attach a thread to hang it from.

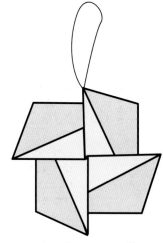

Envelope Closure
Fold four corners of a large square to the centre and insert the inner corners into the pockets behind the inner star.

Spinning Top
To make a spinning top, fold the star version from a small square, 7.5cm (3in) or less, of crisp paper. Extend the creases from the blossom version, steps 4 and 5, through the centre of the inner square to create a spinning point at the centre of the model's base. Crease very sharply and refold into the star version. Place the model on a flat, smooth surface and blow gently from above to spin the top. Usually, the smaller the paper, the better the spin.

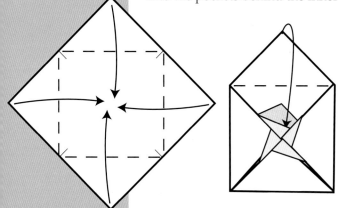

121

folded cards

A folded card combines a card fold (see the Greetings Cards chapter) with an origami decoration. They are either folded from the same sheet of paper, or from multiple sheets joined like a modular.

These cards are great for all sorts of occasions – notes to say thank you, get well, come to a party, save the date, or just to keep in touch.

Look for beautiful papers that will complement the folded design. You may like to produce a set of matching envelopes to make a handsome stationery set for yourself or to give as a gift.

Pinwheel card

It's a card, an envelope, an ornament, a frame and even a spinner!
This simple design offers many creative variations.

Level: Simple.

Paper: Two different coloured rectangles, each in the proportions of 1:2. A rectangle measuring 10 x 20cm (4 x 8in) is a good size. For an insert card, cut a square smaller than one-half of one of the rectangles.

Creator: Kathe Sorg and Gay Merrill Gross (USA).

The card begins as a simple, traditional envelope:

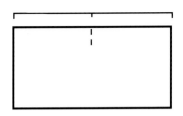
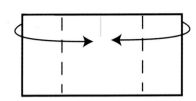
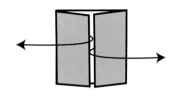

1 Pinch the mid-point of one long edge.

2 White side up, fold the short sides to the centre, leaving a slight gap.

3 Unfold the doors.

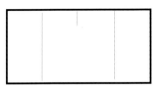
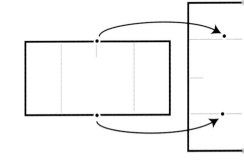

4 Repeat steps 1 to 3 on the second rectangle.

5 Orient the rectangles, one wide, one tall, and centre one over the other, forming a cross.

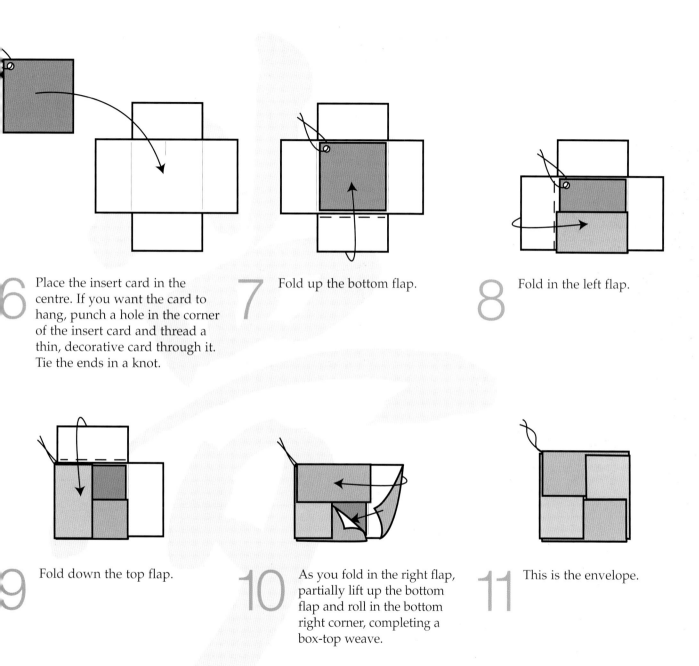

6 Place the insert card in the centre. If you want the card to hang, punch a hole in the corner of the insert card and thread a thin, decorative card through it. Tie the ends in a knot.

7 Fold up the bottom flap.

8 Fold in the left flap.

9 Fold down the top flap.

10 As you fold in the right flap, partially lift up the bottom flap and roll in the bottom right corner, completing a box-top weave.

11 This is the envelope.

PINWHEEL CARD

Use two rectangles of duo paper (a different colour on each side).

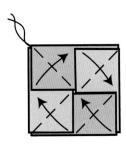

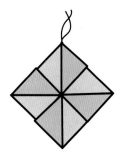

1 Fold the envelope, then fold each loose flap diagonally in half, revealing the inner colour.

2 The finished Pinwheel Card serves as both a decorative ornament, and a wrapper for a message written on an inner insert card.

SPINNER

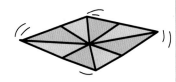

1 To make a simple Spinner, make the model from two small rectangles, such as 4 x 7.5cm (1½ x 3in). Omit the insert card and cord, and fold the finished model diagonally in half in both directions, creasing very sharply to create a pivot point on the bottom on which the model will spin.

2 Place the model on a flat, smooth surface. Flick two opposite corners and the model will spin!

HANGING FRAME

Follow steps 1 and 2 for the envelope. Orient the paper as shown.

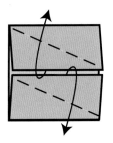

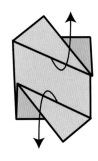

1 Fold the flaps diagonally, from corner to corner, as shown.

2 Unfold the 'door' flaps on each rectangle.

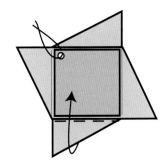

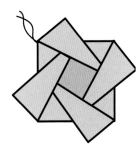

3 Follow steps 5 to 10 for the envelope. For the insert card, use paper of a contrasting colour or a photo.

4 The Hanging Frame can show off a photo or a greeting. You can create your own variations by adding pleats and other folds to these basic forms.

Leaf notecard

Thank-you notes, invitations and get well cards will be all the more appreciated when folded into this lovely leaf design. This model involves narrow pleating, so accurate folding and sharp creases will produce the best result.

el: Challenging.

er: A rectangle in approximate portions of 2.5:1. ectangle of 90gsm lb) bond paper or tionery 10 x m (4 x 10in) uld be ideal.

ator: known.

igin: German der Elke nke received a sion of this design m a friend in rea. She believes it a traditional sign.

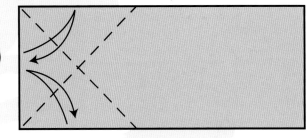

1 White side up, valley-fold an 'X' crease pattern at the left end. Then flip over, top to bottom.

2 Leaf colour side up, refold the 'X', changing the creases to valley on this side.

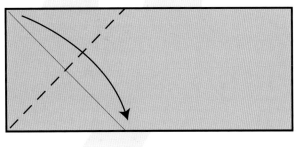

3 Fold the top left corner down to the bottom, refolding on the existing crease.

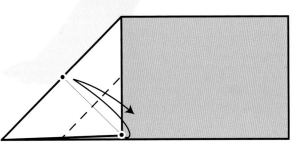

4 Fold the loose corner to the mid-point of the folded edge, crease sharply and unfold.

127

Note Drawings 5 to 14 show only the left end of the paper.

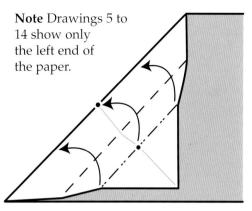

5 Change the valley crease just made to a mountain fold; pinch it upwards into a mountain peak and place the mountain fold on the long folded edge, creating a valley fold midway between the two. Crease sharply.

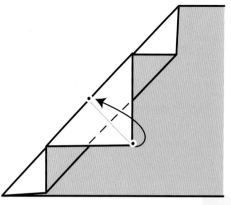

6 Fold the bottom corner to the mid-point of the folded edge, creasing sharply.

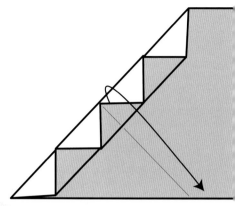

7 Unfold the pleats to reveal the triangular section folded into quarters.

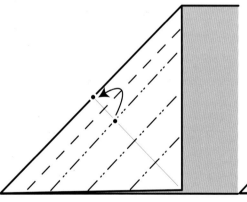

8 Change all of the quarter-creases to mountain creases. Then pinch up the longest mountain crease, forming a peak, and raise it to lie on the long folded edge, creating a valley fold midway between the two.

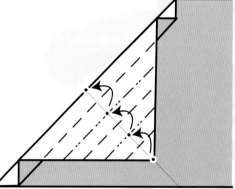

9 Repeat step 8, putting a valley fold in the middle of each quarter-section.

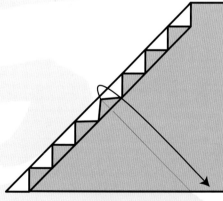

10 Unfold the pleats to reveal the triangular section divided into eighths.

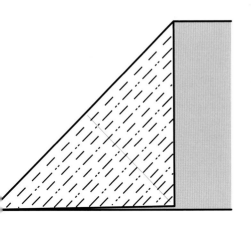

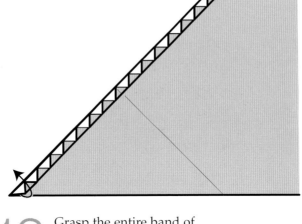

11 Change all of the eighth-creases to mountain creases. (Some already are mountain creases.) Pinch together each pair of adjacent mountain folds, creating a valley midway between the two. This will divide the triangular section into sixteenths, forming a narrow band of accordion pleats.

12 Grasp the entire band of pleats and swing it upwards, unfolding the longest fold (from the original 'X'). The pleats will now be at the rear.

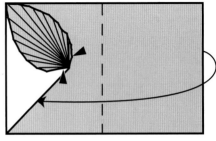

15 Firmly pinch the base of the leaf to secure the folds in place. Tuck the right edge under the leaf design and flatten at the right edge.

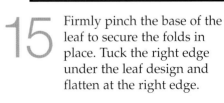

13 Fold up on the existing slanted crease.

14 a) Swing the pleats to the rear.

b) Fold forwards along the vertical cut edge, revealing the leaf.

16 The Leaf Notecard can be paired with the Rectangular Envelope. Fold a set of stationery for a lovely gift.

Bird Card

This clever card is one of my favourite origami designs. It makes a unique, fairly quick card, from just one sheet of paper.

Level: Intermediate.

Paper: A rectangle of medium-weight paper (preferably coloured on both sides). The length can be 2, 2½, 3 or 4 times the width. The height of the card will be the same as the height of the rectangle.

Creator: Didier Boursin (France).

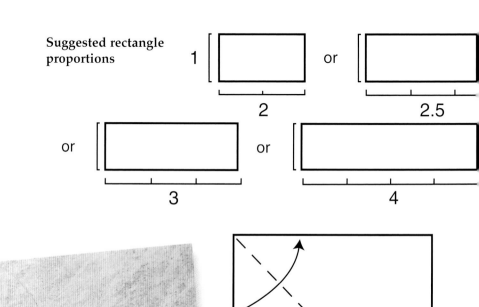

Suggested rectangle proportions

1

2

or

2.5

or

3

or

4

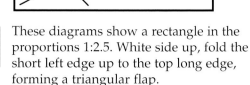

1 These diagrams show a rectangle in the proportions 1:2.5. White side up, fold the short left edge up to the top long edge, forming a triangular flap.

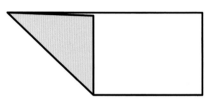

2 The paper now looks like the left half of a boat. Flip the paper over from top to bottom, capsizing the boat.

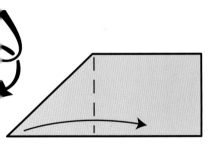

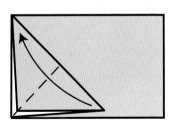

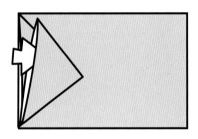

3 Fold the point to the right, bringing the triangular flap to the front.

4 Fold the triangular flap in half.

5 Separate the layers, opening the front pocket.

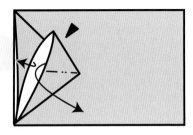

6 Press on the near folded edge, squashing the pocket into a small square.

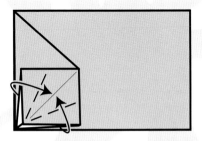

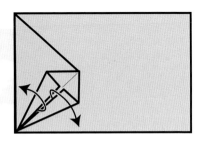

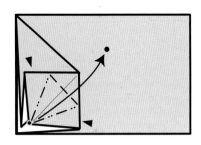

7 Fold the double cut edges of the small square to the diagonal creaseline, as for an ice cream cone fold. Crease very sharply.

8 Unfold the cone creases.

9 Lift the front layer only, creasing a valley fold that connects the two cone creases. Let the cut edges roll inwards, forming a long diamond shape.

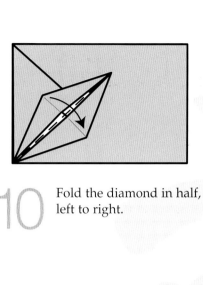

10 Fold the diamond in half, left to right.

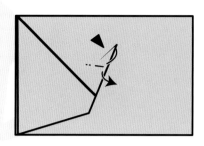

11 Inside-reverse-fold the narrow point to form the bird's head.

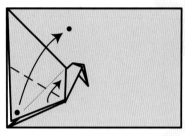

12 Lift the wing upwards.

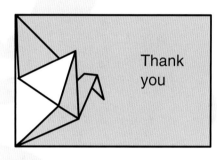

Thank you

13 Write your message on the rear flap.

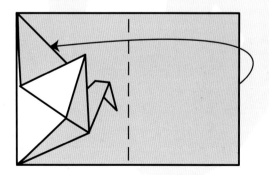 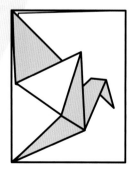

If the length of the starting rectangle was 2½ to 4 times the width, you can fold the message flap in half, and tuck it under the bird.

Star Card

Creator Didier Boursin is the author of many lovely books on origami. This is my variation on his original design. The model can be used as a greetings card, gift tag, or as a place card for a special event. Sharp, precise folds will produce the best result.

el: Challenging.

er: A rectangle in approximate portions of 1:4, h as 6 x 28cm (2½ in) or 10 x 40cm 16in).

ator: Didier rsin (France) and y Merrill Gross A).

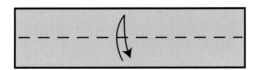

1 Coloured side up, fold in half lengthwise. Crease sharply and unfold. Turn over.

We will be making a series of equilateral triangles on the strip. The folding pattern is: valley, valley, mountain, valley. Steps 2 to 5 show how to do this.

2 White side up, fold the bottom left corner to the centre mountain crease, beginning the fold at the upper corner.

3 Fold the left folded edge to the bottom edge, forming a sharp corner at the bottom left.

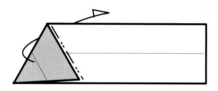

4 Mountain-fold the triangle to the rear, along its right edge.

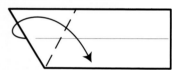

5 Fold the left slanted edge down to the bottom edge.

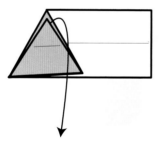

6 Bring the loose top point down, unfolding the triangle into a rhombus (a diamond shape).

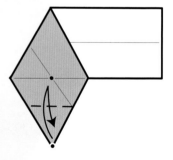

7 Fold the bottom corner to the centre of the rhombus. Crease sharply and unfold.

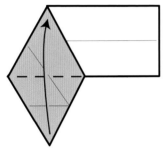

8 Fold the rhombus in half, restoring the triangle.

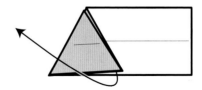

9 Flip the triangle to the upper left, unfolding the crease from step 5.

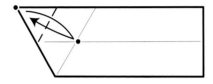

10 Fold the top left corner to the horizontal centre crease. Crease sharply and unfold.

11 Refold on the longer slanted crease.

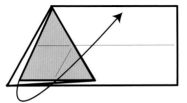

12 Lift the front, loose point at the bottom left, unfolding the large triangle, revealing another rhombus form.

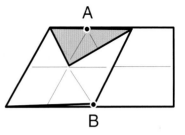

13 Take a straight-edge and place it on the paper, connecting dots A and B.

135

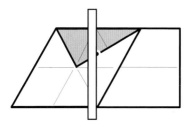

14 Use a pencil to mark a tiny dot where the straight-edge intersects the cut edge. Remove the straight-edge.

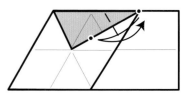

15 The dot you made marks the centrepoint of the large, upside-down equilateral triangle at the right. Fold the right-hand corner of the triangle to the pencil mark. Crease sharply and unfold.

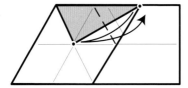

16 Fold the same top corner to the centre of the rhombus. Crease sharply and unfold.

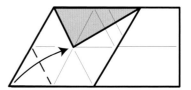

17 Fold the bottom left corner to the centre of the rhombus. Crease firmly.

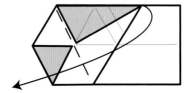

18 Re-lower the large triangular flap.

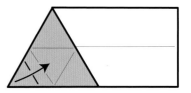

19 Fold the bottom left corner to the centre of the triangle, changing the smaller slanted crease from mountain to valley.

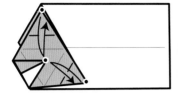

20 Fold the other two corners to the centre of the large triangle. Be very accurate. Crease sharply and unfold.

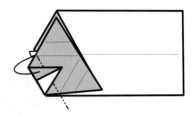

21 Make a flip-out fold by Mountain-folding on the left slanted crease. The short, folded edge will tuck inside the model, as the point on the flap flips out to the side. An interior pleat is formed.

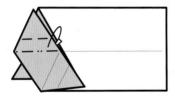

22 Use the existing horizontal mountain and valley creases to pleat-fold the top point to the interior, leaving the point protruding.

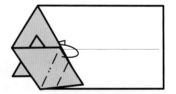

23 In a similar way, pleat-fold the bottom right point behind all layers. This completes the star.

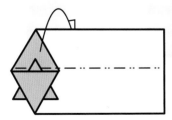

24 Mountain-fold the upper half of the long strip behind the lower half.

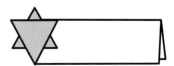

25 The completed Star Card.

Flower Note

Susumu Nakajima's flower is one of the many design possibilities you can make from the Froebel Pattern Fold. We will use it as part of a decorative envelope for a note.

Level: Low Intermediate.

Paper: For the flower use a 7.5cm (3in) square; duo paper or paper shaded at the corners is a good choice. For the envelope use a square measuring 13–15cm (5–6in). A square of 9cm (3½in) memo cube paper can be used to write your message, and then inserted in the envelope.

Creator: Susumu Nakajima (Japan).

1 Make the flower by reversing all the colour instructions on steps 1 to 10 of the Button Flower outer petals (page 99), to give a Froebel Pattern Fold that is coloured on the outside.

2 Blunt the side corners of each little square with mountain folds. Blunt the inner corners with valley folds.

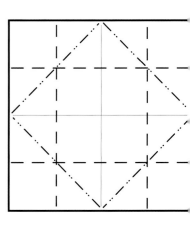

3 To make the envelope, pinch the mid-point of each edge. Use these guide marks to fold all four outside corners to the centre. This is a blintz fold.

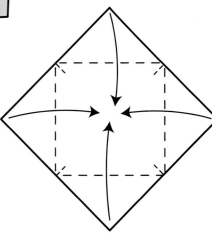

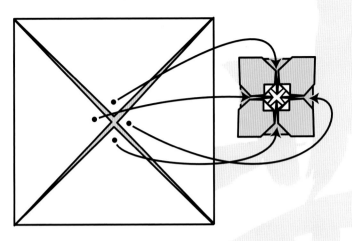

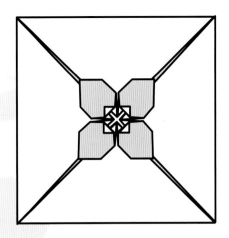

4 Insert your note (written on a memo cube square) under the envelope flaps. Insert each inner corner on the envelope into a pocket on the flower.

5 If the finished Flower Note is a little puffy, press it flat under some books. You may also leave a small gap when folding the envelope corners to the centre at step 3.

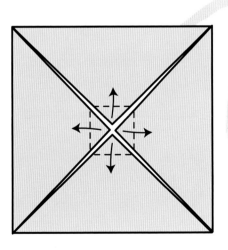

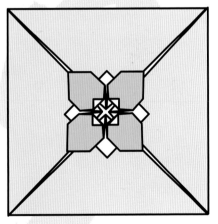

6 If you wish you can blunt the envelope's inner corners to give the effect of a flower with more petals.

7 If you make the envelope from the same size square as the flower, for example 7.5cm (3in), you have a decorative model you can use as a 'tuck-in,' to enclose in a card or letter.

Picture Index

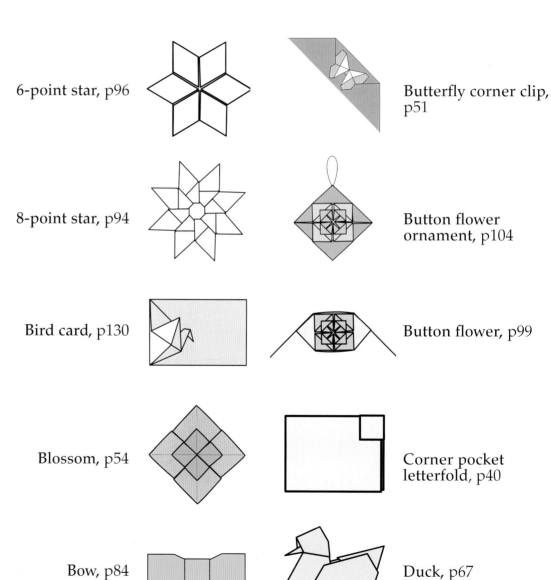

6-point star, p96

8-point star, p94

Bird card, p130

Blossom, p54

Bow, p84

Butterfly corner clip, p51

Button flower ornament, p104

Button flower, p99

Corner pocket letterfold, p40

Duck, p67

Easy envelope, p34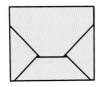

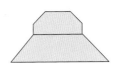 Hat, p76

Fish letterfold, p39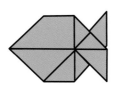

 Layered pocket, p108

Florette, p91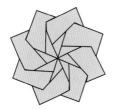

 Leaf notecard, p127

Flower note, p138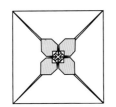

 Leaf, p60

Flower tato blossom, p119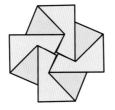

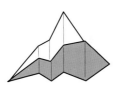 Mountain landscape card fold, p24

Flower tato star, p121

 Party dress, p78

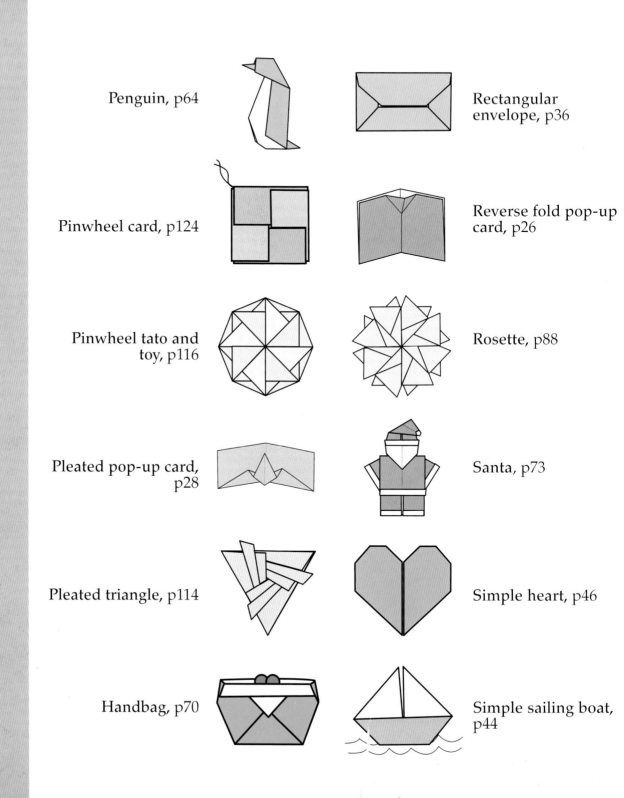

Standing pocket, p112

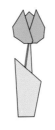 Tulip, p48

Star card, p133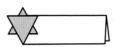

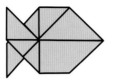 Twist fish, p62

Star wreath, p92

Two-tone dress, p82

Stem with leaves, p58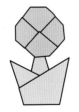

X-cut card with frame, p30

Surprise package, p109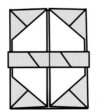

Resources

For more information on origami, including local meetings, international conventions, origami books and paper, contact:

OrigamiUSA
15 West 77th Street
New York, NY 10024
USA
www.origami-usa.org

British Origami Society
Mrs. Penny Groom
2A The Chestnuts
Countesthorpe
Leicestershire LE8 5TL
England
www.britishorigami.org.uk

Acknowledgements

As a child, my mother, father and grandmother were the recipients of my origami greetings. They were the original inspiration for my early efforts at pairing paperfolding with cardmaking.

Through my association with OrigamiUSA I have met many creative and generous friends who have all added to the crafting of this book. I would like to thank all of the creators who gave their permission to include their original designs in this collection.

A very big thank you to Nick Robinson who redrew all of my diagrams on the computer and made this book possible.

Thank you to the staff at Chrysalis Books and in particular, my editors, Miranda Sessions and Marie Clayton.

For beautiful folding papers, thank you to Kotobuki Trading, San Francisco and my generous friends: Tricia Tait, Patty Grodner, Mark Kennedy, Arlene Gorchov, June Sakamoto, Kathy Wallace, Norma Coblenz, Ros Joyce, Sok Song, Pearl Chin, Aldo Putignano, Derek Ettridge, Dorothy Amdur, Elizabeth Couret, Jinni Xu, Kay Eng, Emily Kwan and for the teabag envelopes from Holland – Janneke and Pieter Wielinga.

I am especially grateful to the talented and creative friends who helped me with the card designs: Sok Song (Party Dress, 2-Tone Dress with Hearts, Middy-Collar Dress, Jeweled Purse), Myrna Sigal (Rosette cards), Linda Bogan (Twist Fish and Rosette card), MaryAnn Scheblein-Dawson (Party Dress with flowers card), Kathy Wallace (Florette package decoration) and Mette Pederson (Rosette reversible pin). All other card designs are my own.

Many of the models included in this book were introduced to me by folding friends: Robin Kraut and Anita Barbour (the series of dress models), Lillian Oppenheimer (Simple Sailing Boat), Laura Kruskal (Santa), Tricia Tait (8-Point Star), Kay Eng (Twist Fish), Myrna Sigal (Pinwheel Tato/Toy and Rectangular Envelope), Karen Houston and Dorothy Amdur (Flower Note).

Other models were learned from origami books and publications that were shared by: Tricia Tait, Kay Eng, June Sakamoto, Ruthanne Bessman, Larry Davis, Mark Kennedy, Arlene Gorchov, Linda Bogan and Rachel Katz.

For their assistance in contacting creators around the world, thank you to: Mark Kennedy, Marumi Kurumadani, Michel Grand, Dorothy Engleman, Peter Budai, Sara Giarrusso, Jan Polish, Cynthia Fulbright, Tricia Tait, David Lister, Pascal Ronsseray and Nick Robinson.

Anyone mentioned in these Acknowledgements, I ultimately know because of one person – Lillian Oppenheimer. When she founded The Origami Center of America in 1958, she made it possible for paperfolders around the world to connect with each other, to meet and to share ideas. Starting in 1980, her efforts were continued by Michael Shall and Alice Gray when they founded The Friends of The Origami Center of America, which is now known as OrigamiUSA. Thank you to the current and past Board Members of OrigamiUSA; their dedication has made it possible to continue the exchange of ideas among paperfolders worldwide and to keep this joyful activity forever fun and endlessly creative.

The origami designs in this book are intended for personal use. Commercial use of any origami model in print or other media, requires the permission of the individual creators. For further information contact the author at gay@origami-usa.org.